DANIEL BOONE:
Wilderness Scout

The Life Story *and*
True Adventures *of* *the*
Great Hunter LONG KNIFE
who first blazed The Wild-
erness Trail *through the*
Indian's Country *to* KENTUCKY

NOW FULLY TOLD
BY
STEWART EDWARD WHITE
AND
ILLUSTRATED BY
JAMES DAUGHERTY

DOUBLEDAY, PAGE & COMPANY
GARDEN CITY   NEW YORK
MCMXXVI

D A N I E L
B O O N E:
W i l d e r n e s s   S c o u t

" . . . an inspiring book, one which any
father should be glad to place in the hands
of his growing son. Not only does the story
of Daniel Boone throw light on the early
history of the country, but it inculcates those
qualities that make for real manhood."

The
Literary Digest

The Books of
STEWART EDWARD WHITE

+

Fiction

ARIZONA NIGHTS
BLAZED TRAIL, THE
BLAZED TRAIL STORIES, THE
CALL OF THE NORTH, THE
CLAIM JUMPERS, THE
GLORY HOLE, THE
GOLD
GRAY DAWN, THE
KILLER, THE
LEOPARD WOMAN, THE
MYSTERY, THE
ON TIPTOE
RIVERMAN, THE
ROSE DAWN, THE
RULES OF THE GAME, THE
SECRET HARBOR
SIGN AT SIX, THE
SILENT PLACES, THE
SIMBA
SKOOKUM CHUCK
WESTERNERS, THE

Adventure and Exploration

AFRICAN CAMPFIRES
CABIN, THE
CAMP AND TRAIL
FOREST, THE
LAND OF FOOTPRINTS, THE
MOUNTAINS, THE
PASS, THE
REDISCOVERED COUNTRY, THE

Historical and Philosophical

CREDO
DANIEL BOONE: WILDERNESS SCOUT
'FORTY-NINERS, THE

Juvenile

ADVENTURES OF BOBBY ORDE
MAGIC FOREST, THE

VISION

LIST OF ILLUSTRATIONS

In Color

In Black and White

DANIEL BOONE: WILDERNESS SCOUT

CHAPTER I

WHEN we think of American pioneers we recall automatically certain names—Daniel Boone, Davy Crockett, Kit Carson, perhaps Simon Kenton. Of course there were hundreds, yes, thousands of others, who met the same dangers, exhibited at least approximate skill, fought the same savages. But the names of most of them are unknown: and of the rest only the especial student is aware. Often the more obscure men have performed specific deeds that common legend ascribes to better known names. Columbus, as we know, was really not the first to discover America. Common belief has it that Daniel Boone "discovered" Kentucky; but actually, as we shall see, he first entered Kentucky lured by the glowing tales of a man named Finley who had, with others, preceded him. Did you ever hear of Finley? But we have all heard of Boone.

This is because these men have possessed some quality that the others did not. It did not matter what especial deeds they performed. Others must have performed similar feats, or the West would never have been conquered. Those deeds became renowned, not so much because they were thrilling, but because of the men who did them.

Thus Daniel Boone's name is inseparably connected with the occupation of "the dark and bloody ground" because he was Daniel Boone.

He was one of the many great Indian fighters of his time: lived for years with his rifle and tomahawk next his hand: lost brothers and sons under the scalping knife. He was a master of woodcraft, able to find his way hundreds of miles through unbroken forests, able to maintain himself alone not merely for a day or a week but for a year or more without other resources than his rifle, his tomahawk, and his knife; and this in the face of the most wily of foes. He was muscular and strong and enduring; victor in many a hand-to-hand combat, conqueror of farms cut from the forest; performer of long journeys afoot at speed that would seem incredible to a college athlete. He was a dead shot with the rifle, an expert hunter of game. Other men, long since forgotten, were all these things.

But Daniel Boone was reverent in the belief that he was ordained by God to open the wilderness. He was brave with a courage remarkable for its calmness and serenity. Calmness and serenity, indeed, seem to have been his characteristics in all his human relations. Those who knew him remark frequently on this, speak of the fact that where everyone else was an Indian hater, Boone never cherished rancour against them, so that as honourable antagonists they always met, both in peace and war. He was trustworthy, so that when wilderness missions of great responsibility were undertaken, he was almost invariably the one called. He was loyal to the last drop of his blood, as you shall see in this narrative. He was ready ever to help others. These are simple, fundamental qualities, but they are never anywhere too common; they are rarely anywhere combined in one man: and in those rough times of primitive men they sufficed, when added to his wilderness skill and determination, to make him the leading and most romantic figure. If the Boy Scouts would know a man who in his attitude toward the life to which he was called most nearly embodied the precepts of their laws let them look on Daniel Boone. Gentle, kindly, modest, peace-loving, absolutely fearless, a master of Indian warfare, a mighty hunter, strong as a bear and active as a panther, his life was lived in daily danger, almost perpetual hardship and exposure; yet he died in his bed at nearly ninety years of age.

CHAPTER II

ANY normal and healthy boy would have revelled in a youth similar to that of Daniel Boone. He was the fourth of seven brothers; and was born on the banks of the Delaware River about twenty miles above Philadelphia. His place in history can be better remembered than by dates when you know that he was just three years younger than George Washington. When he was three years old, the family moved up state to a frontier settlement that has since become the city of Reading. Here he spent his boyhood and his early youth, and here he took his first lessons in a school that was to help him through all his life, the Wilderness.

For at that time Reading was a collection of huts situated in a virgin country. People lived in log houses set in clearings that were slowly and laboriously cut out from the forest. They spent their days swinging the axe, haul-

4

ing and burning the brush and logs, heaving out the snarled and snaggy stumps which were sometimes burned, but more often dragged to the boundaries of fields where they were set on edge and so formed a fence of many twisted arms and crevices and holes and devious passageways through which such things as woodchucks or squirrels or ruffed grouse or small boys could slip in a fascinating series of games or escapes. And then the soil must be ploughed and planted. Cattle roamed the woods near by, with bells so that they could be more easily found. These must be brought in every night; and while usually they gathered of their own accord anticipating the reward of a few handfuls of corn, often they must be sought for in the depths of the forest. That was in itself a fine training in woodcraft; for not only must one find the cows, but must not get lost oneself. The clothes worn were spun and woven on the place; every item of food and wear, with very few exceptions, was grown or fashioned at home. Never was there lack of fascinating and useful occupation for the little Boones, occupation that not only developed their muscles but their wits.

For one thing was never forgotten. This was on the border of the Indian country. The little settlement of Reading was not near enough the savages' home country to be exposed to the frequent attacks in force which we in company with Boone shall see later; but it was always in danger of raids and forays by stray war parties from over the mountains. It was settled and inhabited in great part by men who in their youth had fought the Indians. As part of their earliest education the children were taught caution when out of sight of home. The woodcraft of moving quietly in the forest, of trying always to see everything before affording a chance of being seen, of freezing into immobility and silence at the slightest unknown sound or movement until it could be identified was impressed upon them as a mother partridge impresses the same thing on her young.

Nor was there lack of opportunity for practice. Plenty of Indians visited the little settlement. They were "friendly" Indians: that is to say, they were not at war with these settlers and came on peaceful errands. But as Indians they were always to be suspected by a brace of small boys hunting cows in the forest. And so very early in life these children became more expert in observation and more skilful in concealment than anybody could possibly be nowadays, unless he had the same training. No more thrilling, fascinating game of I-spy or hide-and-seek could be imagined than this penetration of the leafy dark forest, every sense alert for every sound and movement; the mind recognizing them instantly—red squirrel scratching the bark, towhee the leaves; the rare weird scrape of a leaning tree rubbing another as the wind touched it; the cautious pad of the lynx as it crossed a patch of dead and sodden leaves; the innumerable disguised voices of wind and water and the cautious conversation of woods creatures—there are a thousand of them; and they all indicate life or movement, and any of them might be a prowling savage, unless one is so familiar with them that he recognizes them for what they are. And when unmistakably that sound of movement *is* the savage, stalking confidently along in the forest aisles with head shaven all but the long scalplock at the crown, painted from head to toe in the bright colours that indicate peace, his black eyes shifting keenly with the perpetual restlessness of the man who lives among dangers, what a triumph to fade so unobtrusively into concealment that the warrior passes unnoticing! There was a zest to this game. For many, many times on the frontier of those days it had happened, in communities quite as peaceful, apparently, as this, that the warrior stalking by had been painted for war —the war paint varied with different tribes: but was most often black with white markings—and that the children searching the woods for the cattle had not managed to escape notice. Then they had been tomahawked or their brains dashed out against trees or carried away. Just such a thing might happen at any time, anywhere. You may be sure that that thought was impressed upon them, until it was always present in their minds. And so, later, when you read of marvellous escapes, feats of woodcraft, wiles of strategy that seem incredible, remember this training from the earliest years.

Later when the day's work was over and the fire was roaring in the fireplace, the elders' conversation had largely to do with the strategy and wiles of Indian warfare. These men talked of it not merely in the way of reminiscence or to tell a tale; but practically. They compared notes and exchanged ideas earnestly, as men would exchange experiences or methods of any job. Thus young Daniel crouched in the chimney corner and listening with all his ears learned of the innumerable wiles and stratagems in which the Indians were so skilful and ingenious; and he learned them, not the way you and I learn them—as curious matters of interest—but as practical expedients to be used in life; much as you now would listen to experts talking about exactly how and where to fish where you are going on your vacation. These items of experience had been bought with blood and massacre. Each trick of the foe had probably succeeded one or more times. Only thus did these pioneers learn to maintain themselves.

Besides the necessity of getting in the cattle were other errands that took our youngsters abroad. In those times were tasks for every pair of hands, no matter how small. We of this age hardly know what poverty is, as these men and women knew it. We may know discomfort and squalor; but we rarely front the danger of famine, for example, face to face. These people perforce travelled life with a light pack. Like the hunter far from his base, they must take every advantage the country offered. Thus the hickory nuts, and walnuts, and beechnuts and butternuts, that to us mean merely a good time in the fall, to them were an essential part of the foodstuffs, and were carefully gathered and stored. That was the children's job. Then, too, there were the berries and wild fruits—blackberries, raspberries, huckleberries, wild plums, wild grapes—which were to be garnered in their proper season; and edible roots. The knowledge of these, together with the possibilities of the inner bark of certain trees, came to these young people, not in the way of play, but in the course of every-day life. Later when it became necessary, as it often did, for them to cut loose from all contact with civilization and to rely on the wilderness for every item of their food, clothing, and shelter,—save powder and lead,—they could do so.

Another phase of this unique schooling was that which is now done by our games and gymnasiums. I refer to the building of their physical bodies. They had pretty good stock to start from. Their immediate forbears were picked men—picked by the energy and restlessness of their dispositions to leave the more contented stay-at-homes and set sail into a new world; picked again from the more settled seaboard by the enterprise and audacity of their spirits to push out into a hard and dangerous wilderness. But in addition to a good heredity they had the advantage of a healthy life. There were privations and even sufferings, to be sure; but in the majority of cases these served merely to harden the fibre. Year in year out the food was wholesome and generally abundant. Besides the game, fish, berries, and other wild products they had cornbread, Indian pudding, maple sugar, milk, butter, and sweet potatoes. Their days were spent in the open air. From the time they could toddle they were given tasks within their strength, all of which required long continued muscular effort. When in their teens they used the axe, drove the teams, lifted at the logs and timbers, held the plough, wrestled with the clearing and the planting of the stubborn soil. As offset to this heavy labour, which might otherwise tend to make them clumsy and musclebound, were their expeditions into the forest; at first, as we have said, after the cattle and wild nuts and berries near at home, later in pursuit of game for the family meat supply. The necessity for wariness, not only to get the game but to save their own scalps, made them as supple and enduring as their home labour made them sinewy and strong.

This physical prowess was further encouraged by the sports of the day. They did not have baseball, nor basket ball nor football. But when boys, or grown men, got together they played games just the same. Catch-as-catch-can wrestling was much in vogue. There were no complicated rules. You just got hold of the other fellow and tried to throw him. Technicalities did not go. It did you no good to prove that *both* shoulders were not on the ground; you were flat on your back, and that was enough. It got you nowhere to flop promptly and then play a defensive game flat on your tummy; you were down, and—what was the real point—your opponent could beat your face in or tomahawk you, were it the real thing. You were licked. They ran footraces, too, at all distances; jumped, both high and wide. One of the most important sports was throwing a knife or a tomahawk at a mark. So, of course, was shooting. About the only real game, as we understand that term, was lacrosse. I suppose you all have a theoretical knowl-

edge of that game; some of you have seen it; and perhaps a few of you have played it.   If not, look it up.   It is sufficient to say here that there is no game that involves more long-continued fast running, is harder on the wind, or that requires more endurance.   When later you read some astonishing stories of feats of running performed by men escaping, or attempting to escape, from the Indians, remember all this early, easy, natural, almost unconscious training. These boys exercised not at stated intervals, or between hours spent indoors, but every day, all day.

One other thing.   They often underwent what to most of us would seem extreme discomfort.   We certainly do hate to be literally wet to the skin.   Often we say we are "drenched through" when in reality we are wet outside and sort of chilly damp in a few places that touch our skin.   But to be really wet through, as when one falls in a river, is to most of us pretty tough and we think we've had a hard time, even when we have very shortly a warm house to go to. These children had no umbrellas, no waterproof coats, no rubbers.   Indeed, their usual foot covering was the deerskin moccasin; and that, as the old-timer expressed it, will wet through two days before it rains.   They were so often wet, so often cold, that early in life they took these conditions merely as annoying but inevitable.   They slept in unwarmed rooms that in winter were so cold that water in a pail or pan would freeze almost to the bottom.   In the morning they had to pile out in that atmosphere, break the ice, and wash.   I am not going to harrow your tender feelings further. These things were not sufferings, were not so very terrible. I do not doubt that a certain number of my readers in the rural districts may be a good deal in the same boat themselves. But *in addition to all the rest* it was hardening and tempering them later to endure. You must understand the way they were raised and the training they had in order intelligently to read of their later adventures.

I am tempted to digress at this point and tell you a story of five of these boys, aged from nine to thirteen years. It has nothing to do with Daniel Boone, except that it shows what this backwoods training can do toward making young lads self-reliant beyond their years.

It was in the year 1785. The two Linn brothers, a boy named Brasher, one named Wells, and another whose name we do not know left home to shoot ducks. They camped overnight near the Ohio River. The fact that they were allowed thus to go alone at a distance shows that the country must have been for some time quiet and that Indians were not expected. However, hardly had they returned from their shooting and lighted their cooking fire when they found themselves surrounded by savages. In spite of the fact that they were completely encircled Linn and Brasher made a dash for it. Brasher was a fast runner and an expert dodger, even at the age of twelve, but he stumbled over a root and was seized. Linn made better progress, and might even have broken through and escaped, but he refused to drop his ducks!

Gathered together about their own fire the Indians proceeded to question them.

"Where you from?" demanded their leader.

"From Louisville," instantly answered Linn, naming a place at some distance in order to conceal the nearness of his own people.

They were marched at a swift pace for many days until they reached the Indian town. Indians on such a journey travel steadily all the day through, without pause. They carry as provisions only corn and maple sugar. Their pace is rapid and over rough country. If any captive lags or falls behind, he is tomahawked. Yet these boys of from nine to thirteen kept pace with their captors.

At the Indian town the women and children rushed out to meet them shouting abuse, pelting them with dirt and sticks, finally approaching near enough to pinch and slap them. The Kentucky boys drew close in a little group. Finally Linn picked out the biggest Indian boy of the lot and knocked him down with a straight left. It appears that as a lead the straight left was a complete surprise to these rough-and-tumble right-handed fighters. That particular Indian boy was so much hurt, or—more likely—so much astonished, that he did not get up; but another promptly flew at young Linn for revenge. Linn licked this one. That was too much. Every youngster in the village piled in. The white boys stood back to back and met them. It was Kentuck against the field. The squaws too tried to mix in the rumpus, but the Indian men, interested in this battle against odds, forbade them. And in spite of those odds the white boys won the battle.

They were adopted into the tribe, and to a boy entered into the life wholeheartedly and with apparent enthusiasm, as though they had no regrets for, had forgotten, their own people. This was dissimulation so well carried out, even by the nine-year-old, as completely to deceive the sharp-eyed watchfulness keen for any signs of grief, homesickness or regret. They took part in the hunting, in the wrestling, the riding and racing. Gradually they gained the confidence of the Indians until at last they were sent on a fishing expedition in charge of a very old Indian and a squaw.

Down the river they consulted anxiously and changed their minds a number of times. To get home they must cross alone many miles of dense forest wilderness absolutely unknown to them. Think how hard it is to keep from getting lost in a very moderate-sized swamp bottomland, and realize what that means. This wilderness, moreover, was full of enemies; and they were certain to be pursued by the most skilled woodcraftsmen as soon as their absence was discovered. They had almost no food; and no weapons except their knives. They were, as we have seen, only boys. Try to think of yourself in their places. Yet their hesitation was on account of none of these things. They were matters-of-course, only to be expected. But they knew that if they were to get clear away it would be absolutely necessary for them to kill the old Indian and the squaw; and that was a dreadful decision for the boys to face.

But it was their only chance. Shortly the tribe would be moving so far away as to make thought of escape hopeless. The deed was done.

It took them just three weeks to reach the river, three weeks in the wilderness without food or shelter other than they could pick up by the way, without other directions than those their wits suggested, and at the last pursued by the Indians. They found their way, they fed themselves on the berries, barks, and roots their education had taught them; they eluded the savages; and so at last came out just where they wanted to be, on the bank of the river opposite Louisville.

Here they shouted until they were seen. But the people of the town were afraid to cross to them. It resembled a very old Indian stratagem. Again and again apparent white people, speaking good English, had appeared on river banks opposite towns or flatboats floating down the current. They told piteous tales of escape from captivity, of imminent pursuit, and begged frantically for rescue before the Indians at their heels should appear and destroy them. No decent man could resist such an appeal. Yet when the flatboat had been swung to the shore, or when a rescue party had crossed from the town, suddenly had up-risen hundreds of warriors, and the decoys among them. A good many massacres had taken place in this manner, enough to make that particular stratagem well known.

So though the boys used every means at their command

to carry conviction, they failed. The river was here too wide to talk across.

"We'll be caught if we stay here," said Linn desperately at last, "the Indians are not far behind us."

They turned up-stream and then, with no other tools than their knives, they set about making a raft. They went up-stream so that when they crossed the current would not take them below the town. They collected pieces of driftwood and down logs small enough to manage, and bound them together with strips of bark. (Would you know, as they did, just which bark would come off in strips at that time of year and would be tough enough to use thus?) The raft was done in a very short time. Four sat on it and Linn swam behind, pushing. So real had been the necessity of haste that before they had much more than reached mid-stream the Indians appeared on the banks behind them! It sounds almost too much like a moving-picture plot; but it is true. The Indians fired at them, and the bullets splashed the water all about them; but they arrived safely.

So when you read, or someone tells you, that Daniel Boone or his contemporaries were "ignorant and uneducated," don't you believe them. Education is the learning of things that fit one for life. These men may have been to a certain extent illiterate in that they did not read many books; but they read life and nature more closely than we ever will, and to greater purpose than most of us will ever read anything. Daniel Boone's spelling was on a free and untrammelled principle of his own, though he could express himself well and clearly; but it was not one per cent. as free and untrammelled as our readings would be of the things that meant happiness, life, or death in his kind of life. He was a very highly educated man; and this is proved by his character, his intelligence, and his wisdom. The value of *any* kind of education is not whether you know more of certain things—book or otherwise—than the other fellow, but what intelligence, wisdom, and character you develop by its means.

One item of this education, and one of the most important, I have left until the last. The entire meat supply of those days came from the wild game. If a man would provide for his family he must be a hunter, and a good one. It is a mistake to suppose that abundance of game always means easier hunting. It may be easier to find where game is, but the individual animal was just as wary then as now, and its successful pursuit demanded as much woodcraft. Besides the usual supply of fresh meat from this source, it was customary also to lay aside each year sufficient dried meat in strips, or "jerkey." It might be interesting for you to know that the word "jerkey" is a corruption of an ancient Peruvian word from the time of the Incas, *charqui,* meaning dried meat. Therefore at proper times of year, in addition to the usual short excursions near at hand, the settlers of those days used to make specifically hunting trips at a distance for the purpose of laying in as much meat as they could to last over the winter. Hunting was not only a sport but a serious occupation.

Fortunately the game was abundant. Deer roamed the forests in herds; bear were incredibly numerous; squirrels and grouse were everywhere; wild turkey frequented the woods in large flocks. Although as yet beyond the reach of young Boone, buffalo and elk swarmed but just over the seaboard mountains. Youngsters were not merely permitted to learn to shoot, nor left more or less to their own devices in the process; they were painstakingly taught to·shoot just as soon as they could lift, however waveringly, the long, heavy rifles of the day. After a certain amount of preliminary instruction the small boy got a licking if he missed; and he was openly shamed if he hit a squirrel anywhere but in the head. At the age of twelve he was made a "fort soldier," and assigned a particular loophole in case of attack.

In all this varied education young Daniel Boone took part and profited. Indeed he may be said to have been a precocious scholar, graduating younger than his mates and with higher honours. He had a true passion for hunting, a passion that lasted all his life and into his extreme old age. In very early boyhood he had a cabin all of his own, built by himself, at some distance from home, where he used to live for considerable periods by himself, for the purpose of better hunting. This most wholesome of sports took him constantly far afield, led him into all the nooks and intricate byways of the wilderness about him, coaxed him into grandeurs and beauties that stay-at-home pioneering could never have shown him. That is what makes the chase of wild animals noble. That is why the man who kills his deer on a still hunt is miles above the one who stops at a salt lick or runway; why he who makes his own stalk can look down on the man who tails a guide. Why is a mountain sheep a trophy and a merino sheep not? Because the former requires skill and knowledge to acquire. If somebody else is furnishing the skill and knowledge, and you are just trailing along and pulling the trigger when you are told to, why not shoot the merino? It means just as much, really: you can make the actual rifle shot as distant as you please. But if you do shoot the mountain sheep, or the elk, or whatever it is, after a guide has done all the real work for you, and you hang its head on the wall, aren't you tacitly indulging in a little false pretence? A mountain sheep head, in a way, is a sort of advertisement or certificate that a certain amount of woodcraft and especial skill has been used to get it. That is the *only* reason why a tame sheep's head is not just as good. If you hang it on your wall, as your trophy, you imply that you had and used that woodcraft and especial skill. Did you? The real aim of sportsmanlike hunting, the real value of the hunting instinct, is not the killing of animals; it is the acquiring of qualities of wisdom and hardihood and patience and knowledge that will enable you to find and kill animals.

CHAPTER III

SINCE the two most important single items in the life and development of those times were the axe and the rifle, and since firearms and shooting are interesting in themselves, it will be amusing and worth while to talk about them a little. I suppose it would not be an exaggeration to say that from cradle to grave one or the other of these instruments was in the hands of any pioneer during fully half his waking hours.

Of the axe there is not much of importance. The American pioneer developed the well-balanced instrument we use to-day. Before him—and indeed in many parts of Europe still—the helve was straight and clumsy. But every frontier farm had to be cleared by chopping, and the wielders of the axes soon refined the old implement to a long, slender affair with a light head. The material was softer than that of our present-day axes. It blunted more easily; but in compensation it could be sharpened readily on stones to be picked up almost anywhere.

As to the rifle, there is the widest misconception. Those

who do not know very much about rifles are quite apt to ascribe impossible accuracy to them. James Fenimore Cooper had a lot to do with that by telling in his Leatherstocking Tales of Hawkeye hitting nail heads at a hundred yards, clipping the heads off soaring hawks, placing one bullet on top of another, and a whole variety of wonderful tales. The tradition has been carried forward by romancers and just plain and fancy liars ever since.

Now item one: you cannot *see* a nail head at one hundred yards; and anybody who can hit what he cannot see is wasting his time when there are so many other miracles to be performed. Item two: there is such a thing as the "error of dispersion." That is to say, if you place any rifle in a machine rest and from it fire a series of shots, you will not find the bullets superimposed one over the other: they will be found grouped very close together, and the diameter of that group is the error of dispersion. This error is due to a number of things, some inherent in the weapon and the ammunition, and some due to temperature, wind, barometric pressure, and the like. The error of dispersion at Cooper's hundred yards for the most accurate rifle ever made would average an inch or two wider than any nail head.

But James Fenimore Cooper is not alone responsible. We get many honestly intended stories of the prowess of "a man I know." One man of my acquaintance used to turn an interesting purple at even an eyebrow raised over his story of an acquaintance who habitually killed running coyotes at eight hundred yards with a 30-30 carbine. I do not know the exact error of dispersion of that weapon at that range but it is somewhere between ten and forty *feet!* And, mind you, in considering only the error of dispersion we are assuming that the shooter sees perfectly, holds perfectly, can estimate distance to a yard, lets off perfectly.

Having thus disposed of the dispersion error as a reason for distrusting the Dick Dead-eyes, we will now examine another little joker called the triangle of error. You lay your rifle across some sort of solid rest; and, without touching it, you look through the sights. About forty feet away you have a friend with a pencil, and a piece of white paper pinned against a box. The friend moves the point of the pencil here and there at your command until the sights are accurately aligned on it. Then you yell *Mark!* and the friend makes a little dot—invisible to you—where the point of the pencil happens to be. He removes the pencil, you remove your eye from the sights, and try it again of course without disturbing the gun. If your eye is absolutely accurate the second pencil dot should be on top of the first. Only it isn't. The triangle formed by three trials is the above-mentioned triangle of error. It measures the variations of sighting your eye has betrayed you into through the fixed sights of an unmoved gun. The size of the triangle will humiliate you. It can be reduced by practice; and it must be reduced by practice if you are to become a good shot; but it will never entirely disappear. Its error must be added to—or, in case of a lucky shot, subtracted from—the dispersion error.

Up to this moment you have not touched the gun, yet already the Leatherstocking feats have been shown to be absurd. Now you must introduce the personal element, the consideration of whether you are a good shot or not. Daniel Boone and his companions were wonderful shots, but they were not perfect shots. No man is that. And this personal error, no matter how small, must be added to the mechanical errors mentioned above. No wonder people get a false idea of the capabilities of rifle shooting, so that when they see some really good shooting it does not seem much to them. And no wonder those who do know something about it come to distrust all the old stories.

But these have gone to the other extreme in their disparagement of the arms of those days. They are willing to acknowledge that the men who used them were wonderful shots, *considering the arms they had to use;* but that with modern weapons they would have been very much better shots. For the old flint-lock rifles of those days they have a good-humoured contempt. They point out the excessively long, heavy barrel, the short, light stock with its scooped butt plate; the simple open sights; and they clinch the matter by calling attention to the flint lock and what they think must have been its slow action, amounting practically to "hang fire." In contrast they show us the modern light, high-velocity rifle with its balance, its aperture or telescopic sights, its true, quick-acting locks, the speed and precision of its percussion ignition. The legend emanating from this body of opinion is that accurate shooting, as we understand it, must have been quite impossible.

Well, let us see.

The typical "Kentucky rifle" looks to us like a uselessly and stupidly clumsy affair, to be sure. It was so long that a tall man could rest his chin on its muzzle when the butt was on the ground. In contrast to its heavy, long octagonal barrel, the stock was short and light, which made it muzzle heavy. The low sights consisted of a plain bar with a nick in it for the rear, and a knife-blade of silver or bone in front. It was fired, of course, by a flint lock. Boone's rifle, which is still in existence, was five feet three and a half inches long, of which the barrel was over four feet. It carried a round ball that weighed 55 to the pound, or 130 grains—15 grains more than a .32 Winchester. As the balls were round, however, the caliber was about 44. It weighed eleven pounds.

Now why did Boone pick that particular kind of weapon? Most people do not realize that there were then plenty of what we call light and handy rifles in existence, and they shot well, too. All sorts of ideas were tried out very thoroughly. There was plenty of opportunity to experiment. If Boone and his companions and contemporaries deliberately chose all their lives to carry eleven pounds of metal, to burden themselves with five feet or so of gun, then they must have had good reasons. As a matter of fact, they did have good reasons.

In the backwoods, remote from all sources of supply,

economy of powder and lead was greatly desirable. It became an absolute necessity when, as did Boone, the hunter cut loose for a year at a time. He should be able to vary his charge of powder according to the distance he had to shoot and the game to be shot. Now a patched round bullet in a barrel with a slow twist is the only sort whose consistent shooting is not affected by great variations of powder charge. A rifle shooting a long or conical bullet must be resighted with any radical increase or reduction of the charge. It will be just as accurate with the new charge, perhaps, but the bullets will hit to the right or left of the old sighting. Increase of powder behind a patched round ball, however, does not affect the sighting at all. It will merely add velocity, and so cause it to shoot farther and hit harder. The sighting does not have to be changed.

Thus the hunter when shooting small game at close ranges would often use but a thimbleful of powder, while for extreme distances he would pour in double! Each man tried out his own rifle with different charges until he knew exactly what it would do. Usually about half the weight of the bullet in powder made a full load. He took the same sight up to about fifty yards with the thimbleful charge that he would at one hundred with the full charge, or a hundred and fifty with a double charge. There is a very persistent legend, which probably you have heard, that they used to measure the powder by pouring it on a bullet held in the palm of the hand until the bullet was completely covered. No such inaccurate method would have been tolerated for a moment by any good shot. When once the proper charge was determined the hunter made him a little charge cup to hold just the proper amount, usually from the tip of a deer's horn, and this was suspended by the bottom (to keep it dry) from the powder horn.

Thus we have found a very good reason for the round ball, and for the fact that the front and rear sights were fixed. They did not need to be moved because the point of aim was always the same: the powder was varied for different ranges, and as there was no increased "drift" it was unnecessary to move them sideways.

But why the very long, thick, and therefore heavy barrel? We are usually told that it was to "burn all the powder." It is a fact, however, that in a machine rest a barrel a foot, or even eighteen inches, shorter is just as accurate. As a matter of fact, the reason is the same as for the round ball: scarcity of ammunition. The aim had to be deadly. It might be added that without muzzle loaders, and without the advantage of our magazines, it was extremely desirable to make the first shot count! And so, again, the aim had to be deadly. It must be remembered that these weapons were developed in a country where most of the shooting was done in the deep shade of forests. Aperture sights were out of the question: and aperture sights are the only sort that do not blur near the eye. Try it. You will find it impossible to focus sharply on the rear sight, the front sight, and the object of aim all at the same time. One of them *must* be blurred somewhat. Usually it is the rear sight, because a slight blur there is of lesser importance. How can this be obviated? By getting the eyes farther away from the rear sight. Try that. Lay your rifle across a table and then look over the sights from a little distance back. Both the sights and the object of aim will be clear and well defined; and naturally that makes for better accuracy. The only way to gain this result is to build a very long barrel and place the rear sight some distance down it. For remember, if you want accuracy there *must* be considerable distance between the front and rear sights. In addition to this consideration there is no question that a strong man can hold a muzzle-heavy gun steadier than he can a muzzle-light gun; and these were all strong men.

Besides, the thick barrel vibrates less than the thin barrel, has less "whip," as it is called. A modern light rifle often has a tremendous "whip," sufficient to throw the bullet far off the mark, but since the whip is always the same it can be compensated for by the sights. If the powder charge is changed, however, then the amount and perhaps the direction of the whip changes, so that your former sighting would be no good at all. That is one reason why reduced charges are so unsatisfactory in modern rifles. But these thick, heavy barrels reduced whip to almost nothing. It was still further reduced by the material from which the barrels were made, a very soft iron, so soft that a shaving could be cut from the edge of the octagon barrel without dulling a knife. The fact that they made the knives showed that they could make harder metal; but this soft iron had less vibration, less whip.

There was also less recoil to a heavy gun. That does not sound important; certainly these husky frontiersmen ought not to have minded that, especially in view of the "kick" we get along with in our rifles. It was not important when the butt was rested against the shoulder. But very often the butt was rested on the upper arm, or even in the crook of the elbow. It enabled the shooter to hold looser and across his body, which made for steadiness: but it was especially practised because he could shoot from behind a tree without exposing more than an eye and his forearm. And that was a healthy thing to do!

The sights were set low on the barrel not only for the obvious reason that they were less liable to injury, but also to prevent the rifleman from "drawing coarse," that is taking in too much of the front sight and hence shooting too high. We do that on purpose sometimes when shooting at longer ranges, but they got the same effect, it must be remembered, by increasing the powder charges. As has been said, the sights were in forest country adjusted for one hundred yards for full charges and one hundred and fifty yards for the double charges. In the open country and in war they made these point-blank ranges longer.

Shooting across the body and from behind trees accounts for the deep scooped butt-plates and for the shortness and "drop" of the stocks. On the right side of the latter was a trap with a hinged brass cover for patches and grease. You may be sure that the brass was never polished! Indeed when the metal anywhere began to show bright it was rubbed with the crushed pod of a green hazelnut or some other vegetable acid. No one wanted a glint of light to betray him to his foes.

The bore at the muzzle was very slightly enlarged to permit of seating the bullet easily, which rested on a greased patch and was rammed home so as just to touch the powder, but not to crush the grains. That is another silly legend, that the bullet must be rammed down hard "until the ramrod jumps out of the barrel." Such a procedure would give an astounding variety of pressures; and our forebears knew better. Home-made linen was used for the patches. It is generally buckskin in the story books; but buckskin was too thick and was never used when linen could be had. It permitted quicker loading, because the bullet did not need to be forced in to make a tight fit; it made a gas check that prevented the gas from getting into the barrel ahead of the bullet; it prevented stripping the ball, and so "leading" the barrel; and it made possible firing many times without cleaning.

The flint lock, of course they used because they had no other. If they could have had percussion they would have been the more pleased. But a properly made flint lock was not too slow for accurate shooting. They are judged mainly by the crude specimens to be found on the old Brown Bess muskets and similar atrocities to be seen hanging on our walls. These had a ponderous hammer with a long sweep, a cumbersome heavy trigger, an appreciable hang fire. *Click—floo—bang!* went they. But the rifles of the hunters were furnished with finely adjustable set triggers that went off at a touch. For the benefit of those who do not know: a set trigger outfit consists of two triggers; when one is pressed it "sets" the other, which will then go off literally "at a touch." Until set, however, it is safe. The spring, lock, and pan all worked smoothly and accurately together, "like too sides of a wolf trap," as somebody expressed it. "The mainspring," wrote the same man, "has an even velvety feel, soft yet quick and sharp. It shot with remarkable evenness. This was due to the fact that the same amount of gas escaped from the touch hole each time it was fired. The touch hole was bushed with platinum and therefore never burned out. And, finally, I never saw this arm misfire. Its owner never used any but the finest French flints, thin and very sharp. They were semi-transparent, and one would fire 150 shots."

That was something all these men insisted on, the thin, clear flint, scraped very fine and clean, and held by very tight-set screws. That, with the other details noted above, practically obviated hang fires.

Another thing they were extremely particular about was the quality of the powder. They made gunpowder in America then, but it was of an inferior quality, consumed mainly by farmers. Occasionally a backwoodsman might employ it on game near home but never, if he could help it, on any serious business. He wanted French powder, with its fine, hard grains of a glossy black. This was quicker and more uniform in action, and when it was used the rifle did not need wiping out so often. Caked powder dirt, as we all know, is fatal to accuracy.

This powder was carried in a powder horn of from a half pound to a pound capacity. It was literally a cow or buffalo horn, but was far from the ugly clumsy makeshifts we see hanging on old muskets. Our frontiersman used to scrape and scrape again until the horn was almost as thin as isinglass. When the grains of the powder could be seen through the horn, it was considered a good job. From the tip of the horn depended by a thong the charger, hung mouth down to keep it dry. Never in any circumstances did they use metal powder horns. They were made even then, but they were used exclusively by the farmer and the military. Powder carried for any length of time in copper or iron is sure to deteriorate because these metals "sweat,"— accumulate moisture at different temperatures. Powder came from the factories in canisters, but was invariably transferred to wooden kegs when it was to be stored for any length of time; or in gourds for lighter transportation. Lewis and Clark had the ingenious idea of carrying their main powder supply in caskets of lead, which does not sweat; and they made the caskets of just enough lead to melt into bullets for the amount of powder they contained. The bullets were carried in a pouch, which, by the way, was called the shot pouch, never the bullet pouch.

With this outfit the first-class shot could not drive nails at a hundred yards, nor superimpose balls one over the other, but he could do excellent shooting. In comparison with what anybody else could do in those days with any other weapon then extant, he did marvellous shooting. Muskets were elsewhere in almost universal use, long smooth bores. Their bore was a little larger than that of a 12-gauge shotgun, and carried a round ball of about 600 grains. If carefully aimed it would hit a mark a foot square at forty yards. At one hundred yards, where Cooper's riflemen were driving nails, about half the balls would go into a four-foot square. At two hundred yards it is on record that an "expert" triumphantly planted a bullet on a mark eighteen *feet* square! This was all very well when all you had to do was to hit a whole regiment in the close formation of that day, but when it came to a squirrel's head or an Indian's eye——!

It is a little difficult to get accurate records, for they did not keep them. The men did a good deal of match shooting, but the proposition was to come closest to a pin point dead centre. A cross was marked on a piece of board, and the contestant pinned over the cross anything he pleased, large or small, to aim at. After he had fired they took down the paper and examined to see how near the centre of the cross his bullet had hit. It is related quite casually of Daniel Boone that at a siege by Indians he shot through the head a man perched in a tree two hundred paces away. That would be excellent shooting to-day. Hangar, a Briish officer, says of the backwoodsman that "Provided he can draw good and true sight he can hit the head of a man at two hundred yards." As you have learned, it was customary to shoot squirrels in the head! Of course, that is close range, from twenty to forty yards. It seems probable that within the limits of their range, even with the "clumsy flint-lock rifles," they held even with the best shots of our day, making up in practice and care of detail what little they lacked in refinement of weapon.

And how they could handle that weapon! Kephart tells of an old-timer who, on request, gave an exhibition of loading. He performed the feat in under ten seconds. This was a percussion lock. Probably a flint lock would be about as fast, for the time necessary to cap a nipple or prime a pan would be approximately the same. It was a commonplace that any hunter should be able to reload at a gallop on horseback, or when running fast afoot. That was no light feat of sleight-of-hand—to pour the powder in the muzzle, ram home the ball, prime the pan. It strikes me that there must have been a lot of powder spilled in the learning!

Of course in the rapid close-range work of a pitched battle extreme care was unnecessary. Speed was much more important. The powder was poured in by guess direct from the horn. The bullets were held in the mouth. Without the greased patch they were small enough to drop down the barrel of their own weight: and being wet with saliva they stuck to the powder and so did not roll out again. But that was for pressure of business. Whenever he had the seconds to spare the frontiersman loaded carefully, and was ready to pick off a foe who exposed no more than an eye or an elbow from behind the tree.

SOAP MAKING

CHAPTER IV

WHEN the young Daniel Boone was about fifteen years old his father decided to move farther south into a newer country. You may be sure Daniel eagerly seconded that move. Although the surroundings of Reading would have seemed wild enough for us, young Boone already knew them so thoroughly that his restless spirit demanded new countries to explore. They trekked across Maryland and Virginia on their journey, probably transporting all their goods in wagons, and accompanied by their little herds. This must have been a delightful journey through a beautiful country, a perpetual picnic of camps by the wayside. They settled finally near a little river call the South Yadkin in the western part of North Carolina.

This was then a region wild enough and rugged enough

to suit any spirit of adventure. Here Daniel grew up to man's full estate in his father's house. There was an immense labour to be performed in building, in clearing, and in planting; and here he rounded out, brought to perfection, the education so well begun. His time was divided between being a farmer and being a hunter; with, however, considerable emphasis on the latter. Plenty of good farmers were to be had, but very few hunters as crafty, as well-informed, and as successful as Boone. To him was confided a great deal of the business of hunting, the procuring of the meat supply, for the rest of the family realized that from a given expenditure of powder, lead, and time Daniel could produce better results than any two of them. And results were what they must have. Sport came second. As Daniel had a true passion for hunting, everybody was satisfied and happy.

In due time other families moved into the neighbourhood. Among them were the Bryans. Within a brief period Daniel met Rebecca Bryan, and within briefer period after that they were married.

The wedding was typical of the day. People came from many miles, sometimes in vehicles, but more generally on horseback. Some had crude saddles of a sort, but many rode quite simply with blanket and surcingle, the women sitting behind and clinging tight to the men's waists. Everybody was out for a good time. The practical joker was in his element. The "road," which was most often a narrow trail through the mountain forests, they blocked by trees felled across it, so that the travellers had either to jump, to make long detours, or to do a little axe work. They tied vines across at a good height to knock off a hat. That does not sound like much fun, but you must remember there were plenty of girls there; and everybody could show off, and help them over the logs, and disentangle them from the vines, and generally skylark about. Sometimes the jokers would make a mock ambuscade, and there would be much firing of blank charges, and shrieks from the girls who would be *so* scared that thoughtlessly they would cling tight to their cavaliers.

After the wedding ceremony there was a grand feast of beef, pork, fowls, venison, wild turkey, bear meat, potatoes, cabbages, and corn bread. Then they danced square dances and reels on the puncheon floor to the squeaking of a fiddle.

The young couple moved farther back into the wilderness, nearer the mountain, and built themselves their home. The neighbours, of course, helped when coöperation was necessary. They called these occasions "raisings." After Boone had cut and trimmed the logs for his house, then his friends gathered with their wives and other womenfolk and bringing their horses and axes. They notched the logs, laid the mudsills, erected the frame of the house, hauling the logs up on skidways to their places. The horses strained, the axes rang, the yellow chips flew, the men shouted. And over in the maple grove the women had fires going and pots bubbling, so that when dinner time came another feast was under way, with the squeaky fiddle not far off before they turned in under the open sky. In this manner the house and the barns and the corncrib went up like magic, so that when these neighbours, shouting their good-byes, trooped away down the forest aisles the Boones had only to chink and roof their new habitations before moving in.

A great deal of frontier work was done in this fashion. It was much more efficient, and loads more fun, to get together. There were "log rollings" when the trees that had been felled to make the clearing were rolled off to the edge of the forest; and "quiltings" when the women sewed together thousands of scraps to make crazy-quilt. When the corn crops had all been gathered and housed, they assembled at "husking bees." They stripped the husks and flung the yellow ears aside to the tune of laughter and again that squeaky fiddle. If a girl uncovered a red ear of corn she must be kissed by the nearest young man. So it was with much of the similar work. Each man did his own job; but also he helped do his neighbour's, and his neighbour in turn helped him. Tasks that would have been interminable, lonesome, and tiresome, thus became pleasant.

As the years went on the little valley of the Yadkin slowly became settled. The smoke from Boone's cabin was not the only one that rose against the mountain. As his neighbours crowded closer it became necessary to set boundaries and limits to his fields. He began to need elbow room.

Some people have written that Boone was a misanthrope, hating his fellow-beings and the world. Nothing could

THE CABIN IN THE CLEARING

be farther from the truth. The writings of those who knew him are filled with his kindliness, his neighbourliness, his charity and wisdom in his dealings with men. But his was the pioneer spirit. He was interested in things as long as they were under construction; but he lost all interest in them when they were finished and ready to be enjoyed. "Something hid behind the ranges" was always whispering to him.

And "something hid behind the ranges" was in this case no mere figure of speech. All the settlement of the Atlantic seaboard had been to the east of the Alleghanies, and had stopped short when that rampart was encountered. Concerning unexplored country that lay beyond, the wildest stories were told. As one little sample: it was told, and believed, that in that land there were snakes with horns on the end of their tails, which they used as weapons. One of these horns, stuck into a tree, no matter how big, blasted it at once! No one knew the truth of them, for none could speak at first hand. There were the dark blue mountains, and their skyline lay sharp against the sunset, but on what the last rays were looking when they sank below this unknown world no man could say.

Out from secret paths occasionally came small parties of Indians bent on trade or sightseeing. They spoke of noble rivers, deep forests, wide plains, abundant game. But they spoke of it also, and fiercely, as a "dark and bloody ground," that no tribe owned or inhabited, but in which all tribes hunted and made war; a country of perils, of certain death, or captivity that would never end. What hope had the white man, no matter how bold and self-reliant, to cross the labyrinth of pathless and frowning ranges, to thread these great forests, to escape or make head against the hordes of fierce beasts and fiercer savages that there roamed? Only a very strong expedition would seem to have any chance at all; and by what means, by what road, could a strong party get there; and how maintain itself when arrived? The foremost minds of the day realized that there lay the country of the future, but the time was not yet.

Nevertheless there it lay, an ever-present lure to the soul of adventure. We can imagine many hardy men, like Boone, smoking their after-supper pipes before the doors of their cabins, looking upon that gilded skyline with longing and speculative eye.

It was a theme of never-ending discussion around the winter fires. No story concerning it was too wild or too absurd. A legend, a formidable legend, grew up about it, its dangers, its beauties, the fertility of its soil, the brilliance of its birds, the swarms of its game, the deadliness of its perils.

To such a man as Boone this legend could not fail to have a strong appeal. The appeal was strengthened not only by the crowding settlement of the Yadkin valley, but by the fact that at this time the exactions and abuses of the officers of the law became very oppressive. The governors sent out from England to administer the colonies were all of the aristocratic class, trained in the traditions of that class, fond of show and luxury, and inclined to appoint men of their own ilk for the lesser offices. By the time that spirit had filtered down to the outlying settlements it had become, petty. Fees were charged by these lawyers and court officials for the most trivial of daily business: one man sued another at the slightest provocation, being urged thereto by these same officials, who would profit by it; and you may be sure that litigation was not permitted to die. The settlers, with increasing ease, began to rival each other in show and ornament. To a great extent the old intimate friendliness of a common danger and a common privation shared was giving way to the more complicated relationships of society. All this irked Boone. He was a man of simple friendliness, simple but true justice, a hearty despiser of scheming or cunning. And, strangely enough, in spite of his long record of warfare later, he was a man of peace, preferring, in spite of a sociable nature, solitude to the wild wranglings about him. But he was a proper pacifist in that he would fight for his own right to be peaceful!

These considerations, strongly reënforced by his adventurous spirit and his love of hunting, were working him toward a climax of resolve. The "something hid behind the ranges" was calling him louder and louder. He might have gone, irresponsibly, at any time, for he was bold and enterprising; but he was not longing for a mere hunting trip. Somewhere in that vast wilderness must be a place where men could live again in peace with each other; in the simplicity of the early days. But not just yet, in the cares of family life and making a living, did the vision form to him as of "one ordained by God to open a wilderness to a people."

CHAPTER V

AT THIS precise moment there drifted into the valley of the Yadkin a man named John Finley who had actually been over the mountains and had come back to tell the tale! He was a bachelor without ties, and he and a number of others like him had formed a hunting party and had traversed a portion of what is now Kentucky and Tennessee. They, like the other wandering hunters and trappers of this and other far countries, were primarily adventurers, out for new game fields, practical men who wanted meat and furs; and they had no interest at all in the possibilities of the country for settlement. The Indians, ignorant as yet that such little advance parties would mean to their country what the white man had meant to the Atlantic seaboard, disdained to attack them.

They returned and you may be sure that in every cabin,

in every crossroads store, their tales and descriptions were listened to with the greatest eagerness. They had been in a country concerning which men's wonder had long been exercised. Before, in the language of Judge Marshall, "the country beyond the Cumberland mountain still appeared to the generality of the people of Virginia almost as obscure and doubtful as America itself to the people of Europe before the voyage of Columbus. A country there was—of this none could doubt; but whether land or water, mountain or plain, fertility or barrenness predominated; whether inhabited by men or beasts, or both, or neither, they knew not."

Now Finley and his friends could resolve some of these doubts. And you may be certain that Boone was one of his most eager listeners. Indeed it is related that he took Finley with him to his cabin, and there kept him for several months as guest, while each evening he listened to the hunter's glowing tales.

Nevertheless, it was not the custom of these men to leap at things rashly. They believed Finley's stories of the richness and attractions of the country and the abundance of the game; but they knew also, by sad experience, the great power of the Indian. Any party of settlers, with the mountains between themselves and the settlements, would have to shift entirely for itself; and then would depend for its very life on the numbers and ferocity of the savages. They knew that while Finley and his party had come through, their safety was due to the fact that they were the first to cross the mountains and the Indians they had encountered had not known what to do. We will discuss later the Indian of that day, but it is sufficient to say here that he was not individually inclined to be unfriendly. Matters of personal revenge, or matters of tribal policy made him hostile. But by now the news that at last the first white men had crossed the mountains from the east would have spread through all the tribes. The elders and the wise men would have heard of it. And these elders and wise men, of the most intelligent of our Indians, would have had time to think the thing over. They could not fail to perceive that a little beginning would end inevitably in the settlement of the whole country. They had seen that happen many times before. So it was extremely unlikely that a second party, even of hunters, would be permitted without pretty careful scrutiny; while an expedition of settlers would take the gravest risks. To the Indian intelligence the stray hunters and especially the traders from the north and northeast were of different portent.

Nevertheless, in the Boone cabin it was resolved that, if possible, a party of men should be formed to visit the new land under the guidance of John Finley. They were to explore, to spy out the possibilities for settlement, to estimate the risks. Then they would return; and, if it seemed wise, organize an expedition of settlers. Incidentally, they would hunt and trap, and the peltries would pay them for their time and trouble. Rebecca Boone listened to these plans and approved. Her sons were by now old enough to take their share of the work; and she was a true frontiersman's wife, ready to do her part.

After much discussion four other men were invited. They were John Stuart, Joseph Holden, James Murray, and William Cool; all steady, courageous men, and graduates of the great school of woodcraft we have described.

They started on the first of May, 1769, selecting a date when the weather was most likely to be good. Since the routes were unknown, they went afoot instead of horseback, as was the custom ordinarily. "Their dress," says Peck, "was of the description usually worn at that period by all forest rangers. The outside garment was a hunting shirt, or loose open frock, made of dressed deerskins. Leggins or drawers of the same material covered the lower extremities, to which was appended a pair of moccasins for the feet. The cape or collar of the hunting shirt and the seams of the leggins were adorned with fringes. The undergarments were of coarse cotton."

They wore leather belts, with the buckles in the rear both to avoid glitter and catching in the brush. The tomahawk was slung on the right side of the belt. The bullet, or "shot," pouch was swung on a strap over the left shoulder and hung on the right side, the powder horn immediately above it. The knife was in the belt on the left side. Each man carried also a small pack containing extras, chiefly powder and lead. They had little in the way of bedding, no extra clothes, no shelters, almost no food, none of the things we take when we think we are "roughing it" severely. The wilderness was to be their home, and from the wilderness they must take all they needed. If it rained, they must contrive a shelter from the materials at hand, or else go wet. If they became hungry, the wilderness must supply them food.

They attacked the journey boldly, and were almost at once cursed with bad weather. All day they had to travel in the rain, through wet brush that soaked them even more thoroughly than mere rain could ever do. Near nightfall they made their camp. For this they selected a big down-log on a flat space, cleared out in front of it, set upright forked poles with a cross pole seven or eight feet from the logs; laid other poles from the cross pole over to the log: on them placed bark or skins or anything handy that would shed water, and so became possessed of a lean-to shelter that would keep out the rain. The big down-log was the back wall, the height of the forked poles in front determined the slant of the roof, and that was arranged not only best to shed the rain, but also most effectively to reflect down the heat from the fire. Both in the location of the fire and in the building of it they took the greatest pains. Camp was always placed in a secluded hollow, or in a thicket whence, under the most careful scrutiny, no gleam of light could escape. When in imminent danger of Indians sometimes no fire at all would be made, and the men would lie close to each other for the sake of warmth, but as they had almost no blankets at all, this was avoided whenever possible. The fire was urgently needed, not only for warmth and for cooking, but also to dry out daily their sodden belongings. From the slanting roof the heat reflected downward. It is astonishing how comfortable one can be in these circumstances even in the coldest weather and with but a single blanket.

However, it did not rain all the time. One month and seven days after they had left the valley of the Yadkin, late in the afternoon, they struggled up the last ascents of the formidable mountains and looked ahead to the west. The skyline of a hill has ever a remarkable fascination: always one is eager to see what lies beyond, and almost invariably one hastens his steps as he nears the point where he can see. Imagine the eagerness of these men who were at last, after five weeks of hard travel, to look upon a new and strange land!

They had come out opposite one of the headwaters of the Kentucky River. Immediately at their feet, of course, rolled the billows of the lesser ranges and of the foothills, but creeping out from that and rising to the horizon opposite their eyes lay a rich and beautiful country of forests and openings, of low hills and vales, and a vast level plain. The details were lost in the golden mist of evening, but enough could be seen to justify Finley's tales. Long they stood, leaning on their rifles, gazing in a muse of speculation or anticipation each after his desires. Perhaps it was from this high point that Boone received his inspiration that he was ordained by God to open an empire to a people.

They camped that night in a ravine that headed near by.

DANIEL BOONE: WILDERNESS SCOUT 49

Early next morning they descended excitedly to the lower country.

What they found exceeded their wildest expectations. As hunters they were most of all interested in the game. Turkeys were so numerous that Boone later described them as being like one vast flock through the whole forest. Deer were in herds. Elk roamed the woodlands. Bear were, next to deer, the most numerous of all. But the buffalo amazed them most. As our party descended the mountains they became aware of a dull, continuous rumbling sound that puzzled them greatly. They found that this sound came from the trampling of innumerable buffalo. "We found everywhere abundance of wild beasts of all sorts," said Boone himself. "The buffalo were more frequent than I have seen cattle in the settlements: sometimes we saw hundreds in a drove, and the numbers about the salt springs were amazing."

They picked a site on the Red River, built themselves a small rude cabin, and proceeded to hunt and explore the country.

From the first of May until the twenty-second of December they roamed without seeing even an indication of Indians. All this region was claimed by Cherokee and Shawanese, but with none too good a title. As a significant fact no Indians at all inhabited it. Their villages were many days' journey distant, and they themselves visited it only on hunting or war parties. This fact made it a continual battleground when enemies were encountered.

Whenever villages were near at hand, the Indians had either to keep peaceful or to go to war in good earnest; for their homes lay open to reprisals. But if those homes were so far away as to require a long journey before a counter blow could be struck, the smallest parties could get up little wars of their own.

The bales of peltries grew in number. All through the summer the hunters lived literally on the fat of the land. Kentucky before the days of cultivation was as fertile, though in a different way, as she is now. The forests were high and beautiful with flowers and vines and birds; the canebrakes luxuriated; the plains were sweet with clover; the open woods were like orchards carpeted with grass. Everywhere the game roamed. His companions would have been content to hunt close about the little cabin, for the game was as abundant there as farther afield, but Boone had other things in view besides hunting. He wanted to see what the country was like. Always in the back of his mind was the thought that some day he would be returning with his family, at the head of an expedition of settlers. He wanted to examine for himself the possibilities. Ever in view he kept the requisites of what he sought. For a good location in those days he needed to find a gently sloping swell of land on which thickly growing cane, pawpaws, and clover indicated good soil. The trees round about must be abundant enough for building purposes, but should stand sparsely enough, and free enough from underbrush so that a man could ride horseback through them at least at half speed. A grove of sugar maples should grow not too far away; and a salt lick was desirable. Salt did not come in cartons then, but had to be boiled from the water of salt springs. An ideal site should have a good limestone spring so located that it could be enclosed within the stockade walls; but this was not absolutely essential. Many writers wonder why forts were ever built without enclosing springs and they point out several celebrated instances where the besieged inmates were starved for water. At first thought it would seem essential; but these men were thoroughly acquainted with the Indian character. An Indian siege rarely lasted longer than a day or two at most, and ample reservoirs were supposed to be kept filled for such emergencies: though sometimes people got careless through long immunity and neglected to fill them. It was very difficult to find sites suitable in other ways and also possessing such springs.

In this prolonged wandering they had many adventures. One of the most exciting occurred one day as they were crossing an open plain and encountered a great horde of buffalo. The animals were frightened by something and came thundering down in a dense mass directly toward the little group of hunters. To the five newcomers there seemed to be no escape; but Finley, who knew something of these animals, with great coolness shot one of the leaders dead. Like a stream about a rock the rushing herd divided around the dead buffalo, only to close in again as the pressure forced them together. But as that did not happen immediately a narrow clear space was left, and into the centre of this our hunters immediately advanced. There they stood while, with a thunder of hoofs and a cloud of dust, the fear-crazy animals swept by.

The continued absence of any sign of a foe at last lulled them to a feeling of sufficient security so that they divided into pairs for their hunting trips instead of all six staying together as heretofore. Everything went well until December twenty-second. On that date Boone and Stuart were hunting in the canebrake country. This was so thickly grown that it could be penetrated only by means of the buffalo trails; or *streets* as they were called because of their breadth. Some of these streets had been used for years and years. This type of country was especially adapted to ambuscade, and it is extremely probable that Boone and his companion would not have ventured into it had they had any intimation that Indians ever visited that part of the world. However, just as they were surmounting a little hill, a large party of Indians rushed on them so suddenly that they had no chance even to throw up their rifles for a shot.

It is the universal testimony that no circumstances ever ruffled Boone's temper or judgment. He submitted with apparent good humour, and advised Stuart to do the same. The whole party started off at a rapid gait through the forest. Boone knew the Indian character well. He was perfectly aware that only a fearless bearing, an apparent contentment with his lot, and complete patience would help him. Even in later days, when warfare between white and red became embittered, and when he himself had acquired reputation with the Indians of being a formidable enemy, Boone seemed always to command an enormous respect from and influence over them. For all their ferocity in war, the Indians of that day and place responded readily to fair treatment or generous nature. Boone fought Indians all his life, but he never hated Indians. He understood their minds thoroughly, possessing the rare faculty of being able to take fully their point of view and to know what was going on in their thoughts. He must, too, have been an actor of considerable ability, for in his various captivities he never seems to have failed to impress the savages with the apparent sincerity of his desire to become one of them. That was always his first move toward escape; the building up of the idea that he was contented with his lot, that he was on the whole rather glad to have been captured, that he intended to become a member of the tribe and to settle down contentedly with them. Somehow, as we shall see, he always did manage to avoid death, even when the Indians were killing all their other captives; and he always did manage eventually to escape. The former was probably to a great extent due to the placidity, the courage, and the unruffled benevolence of his character; the latter to his great patience, for he never tried to get away until the time seemed ripe. An unsuccessful effort to escape was certain death. The Indians looked upon it as a breach of hospitality, a bitter offence, that a captive they had treated kindly should make such an attempt.

Therefore Boone, and on his advice Stuart, went with their captors cheerfully. So well did he ingratiate himself in every way that the savages were fully convinced that he really wanted to become a member of their tribe; and promised to adopt him. At first guards were set over the white men every night, but by the seventh day their suspicions were so far lulled that they dispensed with that protection. It is evident that this was a hunting party, and not a war party out for scalps and prisoners, or the white men would have been better guarded. They had been picked up in passing. On this night the guards for the first time were omitted, though Boone and his friend were each made to lie down between two Indians. Stuart promptly fell asleep, for he was depending on Boone to judge the right time. About midnight, when the fires were flickering low, the night at its darkest, and the Indians sleeping most soundly after an especial feed of roasted buffalo meat, Boone cautiously raised himself on his elbow. An Indian stirred; he dropped prone again. The second attempt was more fortunate. He touched Stuart, who was instantly broad awake. The two men rose by inches; by inches moved across the little camp. The Indians were lying all about them, men accustomed to midnight alarms sleeping "with one eye open," alert to spring to wakefulness at the slightest sound. The breaking of a twig, even the sudden rustling of a leaf, would have been enough to bring them to their feet, tomahawk in hand. But the two managed it, they succeeded even in regaining their rifles and equipment; and once outside the circle of the firelight they made their way as rapidly as possible back to their camp. There is no record of their being pursued, as they would certainly have been had this been a war party. Probably their escape was not discovered for some time, and it was considered too much trouble to back track on a long and laborious pursuit.

But when they reached the cabin they found it ransacked and their companions gone. All the peltries, result of eight months' work, had been stolen. Their four companions, including Finley himself, were never heard of again. They may have been killed or carried off by the Indians who plundered the camp; but if so nobody ever heard of it in later years, and as a usual thing such victories are boasted of by the Indians. They may have perished in the wilderness, attempting to regain civilization. No one knows. One account purports to tell of their return to civilization; but I have been unable with the documents at my command to trace it. It would seem that such a return would have brought the news of Boone's capture, which does not appear to have been known.

Most men after such an experience would have themselves given it up as a bad job; but Boone and Stuart, instead of being discouraged, resolved grimly to start all over again. They could not afford to return empty handed; for in order to make this journey they had gone into debt. They built themselves a small hut in another and more secret place, and patiently set about retrieving their fortunes.

It might be well to tell here that the main object of their

hunt in the past summer had been deerskins. The pelts of the fur-bearing creatures are not good at that time of year, but buckskin is always in season. Roughly dressed deerskins were worth about a dollar each and a horse could carry about a hundred of them. You must remember a dollar then was worth many of our dollars now. In winter beaver and other pelts could be had, worth from three to five dollars. Buffalo hides, bearskins, and elk hides were fine for bedding and warmth in camp, but they were too bulky to carry long distances. The deer season was over, but beavers and others were coming in, and the hunters could now profitably turn themselves into trappers.

Their outlook was none too rosy. Ammunition was by now getting very low. The Indians had at last shown themselves, and were known to be abroad in the country. Fortunately the fur-bearing animals they were now to take would be captured by traps, so they could save their precious powder and lead for food and defence.

In January Boone saw in the distance two men riding through the woods. He hastily concealed himself.

"Hullo, strangers, who are you?" he called at length, as he saw they were but two.

"White men and friends," hastily replied the newcomers.

They approached and Daniel, to his great joy, found that one of them was a younger brother, Squire Boone. Squire, in company with another adventurous spirit named Neeley, had started out to find his brother, and had succeeded!

This was at once an admirable piece of woodsmanship

and extraordinary luck. He had not the slightest idea of where to look: he just started out; and his journey was just as bold, just as exploratory, just as indicative of highly specialized education as that of his older brother nearly a year before. Indeed it was even more courageous, for here were but two men where had been six. Many writers have expressed the greatest wonder that the two parties encountered at all, pointing out that the wilderness is not supplied with a guide book, and that there was no one from whom to enquire. It was indeed good luck, and went far to justify Boone's faith in his destiny; but to a woodsman it is not as extraordinary as would at first appear. Squire undoubtedly knew where his brother had started, and perhaps his route for a certain distance. In a mountain district the "lay of the land" is generally so strongly marked that the best route and the best passes are inevitable to the eye of a trained man however confusing the choice might be to one less experienced. So Squire, having started right, was almost forced by the common sense of the situation to follow the route taken by Daniel. It is also extremely probable that the latter had marked his trail for future reference, though it is not likely that he blazed it plainly to his front door. That would be asking for trouble, and fairly inviting the foe to visit him.

Squire brought with him ample ammunition and supplies. The four men, delighted with this change in luck, took up their hunting again. Daniel and Stuart held together, while Squire and Neeley struck partnership. The pairs would often go on expeditions lasting for several days at a time, visiting wide-flung trapping routes, or exploring new country, which was as you may imagine a never-failing source of delight. During these expeditions the two men in turn would often separate for the day, meeting at sundown at some agreed spot for the night's camp. One night Stuart did not appear. Boone, in alarm, searched the forest. He found at length traces of a fire where his friend had spent the night but no sign or trail of the man himself. Five years later he came across Stuart's bones in a hollow sycamore tree. He knew them for Stuart's because of the name cut on the powder horn. What happened has always remained a mystery. From the fact that the bones were in a hollow tree, is likely that he had been wounded badly enough to die while in hiding.

At any rate, this mysterious disappearance frightened Neeley so badly that he decided he would start for home, which he did. He would have done better to have taken a chance with the brothers, for he never was heard of again: unless an unidentified skeleton found years later may have been his.

Daniel and Squire Boone settled down to mind their traps and gain enough pelts to pay their debts. They took every precaution against the Indians; and successfully. A new cabin was constructed in a more secret place. All cooking was done at night, so no smoke was ever visible. The trail to the hiding-place was carefully blinded by all the devices known to them. For example, part of the approach was made by walking in the stream; on the ground the trail often turned at angles; or doubled back on itself so that apparently it led nowhere. When possible it was taken over rocks or smooth down trees that would show no trace. One device was to swing on the tough hanging wild-grape vines. Always, when anywhere near home, the footprints were painstakingly covered with leaves. This was a lot of trouble, but these men were protecting their lives, and no trouble is too much for that.

When spring came they had a good store of pelts, but again ammunition was running low. By the flickering little fire, carefully guarded and screened, they held many anxious consultations. They might both return, and as Daniel missed keenly his wife and children, this appealed to him most. But, on the other hand, he had gone deeply in debt to make possible this expedition. Furthermore, it was extremely desirable, if later he was to settle in the new land, that he explore it farther afield; something he had been unable to do thoroughly while the main job was hunting. So finally it was agreed that Squire should return to the settlements for supplies, and to sell the skins, while Daniel should remain. On May first Squire started. The distance was five hundred miles of howling, dangerous, uncharted wilderness, which he was to traverse alone and burdened with the handicap of laden pack horses. It is hard to tell whose courage most to admire: that of the man who stayed, or that of the man who went.

CHAPTER VI

LEFT thus alone Boone acknowledges quite simply that
he "passed a few days uncomfortably." "I confess," said he, "I never before was under greater
necessity of exercising philosophy and fortitude. A few
days I passed uncomfortably. The idea of a beloved wife
and family, and their anxiety upon the account of my absence and exposed situation, made a sensible impression on
my heart." In another place he says that he was "one by
myself—without bread, salt, or sugar—without company of
any fellow creatures, or even a horse or dog."

But he soon shook off this depression. Boone was a profound lover of nature and of her beauties. He "undertook
a turn through the country" as his stilted amanuensis makes
him express it, "and the diversities and beauties of nature I met expelled every gloomy and vexatious thought."
As ammunition was now scarce and so, except for food,
hunting was impossible, he spent his time in exploring,
"for to look and for to see." There was no object in stay-

ing near the little cabin; indeed there was every reason for avoiding it. Alone in a hostile country, where news of the presence of these white men had by now spread to all the tribes, he must take extra precaution against the Indians. He changed his habitation frequently, living in camps of bark or boughs, or in caves. Even in such temporary quarters he rarely ventured to sleep, retiring some distance into the thickets and dense canebrakes unless the weather was very bad. It was a hard and dangerous life, but it had its compensations in the thrill of solitary exploration, the dangers avoided, and the beauty of the new country whose features were thus discovered. Boone wandered far over the thickly forested hills and valleys, the wide plains. He found and followed watercourses; he climbed high hills to look abroad; he revelled in the flowers; in the stately and beautiful trees in their great variety—the sugar maples, the honey locusts, the catalpas, the pawpaws, all the hardwoods; he visited the mineral springs that have since become famous, Big Lick, Blue Lick, Big Bone Lick, where he must have looked with interest and awe on the remains of mastodons down and perished centuries before when they had come to the licks for salt. During these months he gained the intimate first-hand knowledge of the whole country which later was to prove so valuable to himself and to others.

The only person who could have told all the details of this most fascinating solitary sojourn in a new land was, naturally, Daniel Boone himself; and unfortunately he has not told much. He was of few words. Seven years later a man named Filson purported to put down "in Boone's own words" an account of the Hunter's life; but the words were Filson's, and Filson was highflown, not to say elegant. The following is his idea of how Boone would express himself:

"Just at the close of day the gentle gales retired and left the place to the disposal of a profound calm. Not a breeze shook the most tremulous leaf."

Filson had the advantage of getting the facts from our Hunter, no matter how fantastically he dressed them; only unfortunately Boone had a habit of passing casually over a five-hundred-mile journey full of dangers, difficulties, and escapes with the statement, "I returned safe to my own habitation." So of the many things it would be interesting to know of this exploration we have very little. We can never know how many times Boone encountered Indians, nor how many times he managed to elude them. We know that once he met a large band near the Ohio River, but managed to keep out of sight. On another occasion he came upon an Indian fishing from the trunk of a fallen tree. Nobody knows the circumstances; but Boone, in telling of this incident later, would remark gravely but with a twinkle deep in his eyes: "While I was looking at the fellow he tumbled into the river and I saw him no more." Boone was at that moment, in all likelihood, "looking at the fellow" over the sights of his rifle! Again, while he was exploring a new and strange river, he found himself suddenly

THE LEAP FROM THE PRECIPICE

faced on three sides by his enemies. The fourth side was a precipice sixty feet high. Without a moment's hesitation Boone made the leap, landed in the top of a sugar maple, slid down the trunk, ducked down below the cut bank of the river, ran along the little beach there, plunged into the river, swam across and so escaped from the astounded Indians. It is to be noted, as additional evidence of his coolness in danger, that he retained throughout his grasp of his five-foot eleven-pound rifle. He says that during his absence his cabin was several times visited and ransacked.

About the time he had reason to expect the return of his brother he came in from his wanderings. The latter part of July Squire Boone appeared, having for the third time accomplished the difficult journey undetected. His arrival was most cheering. In the first place, he brought news of Daniel's family and that all was going well; in the second place, he reported that he had made a favourable sale of the furs, and had paid off the whole debt; and in the third place he had brought two pack horses laden with supplies.

The brothers opened another season against the deer. It was highly successful, so that in a very short time Squire was able to pack up the horses and once more head out for the settlements full laden. This time he made the round trip in two months, again without molestation. In the science of woodcraft he seems to have been quite the equal of his more famous brother. By December he was back again, and the two entered upon another winter of combined trapping and exploration. They did more of the latter this winter. They had horses; and they were now fully determined to bring settlement to this beautiful land. Boone says himself that he "esteemed it a second Paradise." It was in March of this winter that they finally determined the site of their future home on the Kentucky River. Shortly after, convinced that at last he knew all that was necessary to know, Boone turned his face homeward.

CHAPTER VII

BOONE'S return was like the return of Columbus. The legendary land over the mountains had been entered by someone people knew. He could tell what lay behind the ranges. He had not only visited that land, but he had maintained himself successfully in it for two years. The impenetrable mountains had been crossed, not once, but several times, so that it might fairly be said that a route had been established. From being a dream, that strange far country had become a possibility. Men wanted to know about it in detail. Boone's statements and opinions were eagerly sought and listened to, and his opinions were weighed.

But when it came to action there was a good deal to be thought of. The Boones had lived there and returned, to be sure: but where were Finley and Cool and Holden and Murray and Stuart of the original six? And where was the man who had started out with Squire Boone? It was one thing to go into a country as a hunter, lightly equipped, mobile. Such was able to dodge and skulk and hide; and in any case was never the object of any determined effort by the Indians. If he fell in their way, he was likely to lose his scalp; but they would not bother especially to hunt for him. But settlement was a different matter. It offered a definite point of attack. And furthermore the Indians knew very well from experience that settlement meant that sooner or later they would be crowded on, and they were on that account hostile to anything like permanent occupation. No matter how attractive the picture or how much a brand-new game country appealed to these bold men, there was a lot to be thought of before one sold his farm and ventured.

Two years passed before Boone made the move. In that period, however, he several times visited Kentucky, alone or in company with two or three companions, partly for the purpose of further exploration, but mainly to enjoy his favourite sport of hunting. Other parties of hunters also went in. Many of these marked with their tomahawks possible farm sites. One party, called the Long Hunters, were just making camp for the night when they heard a "singular noise proceeding from a considerable distance in the forest." The leader told his men to keep perfectly still and he himself sneaked carefully from one tree to another toward this "singular noise." He was thunderstruck to find "a man bareheaded, stretched flat on his back on a deerskin spread on the ground, singing merrily at the top of his voice." It was Daniel Boone who was whiling away the time waiting for his brother, Squire. The report does not seem to be a very high testimony for Daniel's singing!

He and his companions had many interesting adventures in this free gypsying around. There was no formal Indian war on, but in the "dark and bloody ground" every man's hand was against every other's. As we have said before, there were no Indian settlements in Kentucky; but there were swarms of hunters and raiders. The villages were all at a distance. There was no need, therefore, to conciliate the whites, as they had to do when the villages were near enough to suffer retaliation. On the other hand, the Indians could never carry on a very long war at a time because they were so far from their base, which made it easier for the pioneers.

In this situation it happened that two white hunters had their camps a few miles apart, but without knowing it. One day they caught sight of one another, and promptly sprang behind trees. In the usual fashion of Indian combat they advanced, darting from tree to tree, trying to get a shot, but trying equally not to expose themselves. This went on for about three hours with neither man getting the advantage. They were equally skilful at this fascinating game that meant life or death. Every stratagem known was used to draw the other man's fire without too much danger of getting hit.   Whoever shot first and missed was of course at a big disadvantage.   Before he could reload his flint lock the other man would be upon him.   At length one became impatient over this long-drawn, futile manœuvring.

"Come out of that, you 'tarnal redskin!" he shouted.

"Redskin yourself!" retorted the other.

And then they had a good laugh and joined forces; for they each agreed they had never before met any one so skilful at "Injun fighting."

Every precaution was always taken against surprise, yet in the dense forests, and in unusual conditions of wind and weather, surprises would happen.   One day Boone and his small party of hunters were eating lunch when suddenly about fifty feet away appeared a large party of Indians. Both sides were equally surprised here, and neither wanted to start anything.   With an assumption of indifference, and as if that was what they had intended right along, the Indians squatted down and began to eat *their* lunch.   There the two parties sat, eyeing each other, neither wanting to make the first move.   Finally Boone arose and sauntered over, picking a bone.   He greeted the Indians, who answered cautiously.   Then he asked to look at a curious knife one of the Indians was using.   The warrior handed it over.   With the intent black eyes focussed upon his every movement Boone apparently swallowed the knife, produced it from his shirt, and handed it back.   With a howl of dismay the Indian threw it as far as he could into the brush, and the whole party disappeared.

Another time the situation was reversed.   A small party of Indians met a larger party of whites.   Before the latter could fire the Indians began to cut up the most extraordinary monkeyshines, running in circles, crawling about on their hands and knees, hopping fantastically about, standing on their heads.   So imbecile was this unexpected performance that the white men stared at them bung-eyed in astonishment.   And before they could recover their wits, the Indians one by one had faded away.

Boone had the great gift of patience.   Two years he had spent in his almost solitary explorations, and now again he was willing to wait.   There is no use in rushing things to failure.   Willing to take the most terrible chances when it seemed necessary, he believed in having things as near right as possible before he started any big project.   It would be all well enough to take his family in and establish it; but defence, companionship, and above all the fulfilment of his dream demanded that others should accompany and follow him.   So patiently he made his calm recital over and over, forming public sentiment until at last in September, three years before the beginning of the Revolutionary War, Daniel and Squire Boone and their families left their old home. Farther along toward the mountains they were joined by five other families.   The party was now a strong one. There were forty men, well armed.

They had with them the materials for permanent settlement—pack horses, cattle, milk cows for the children, swine, seeds, the simple household utensils of that time, including now full-sized axes instead of the tomahawks the explorers had used. For bedding they carried blankets and quilts where the hunters had been content with skins. To be sure this does not seem like great luxury, especially when we consider that wooden plates and platters and gourd cups were in exclusive use on the table. The hunters of the families used their hunting knives, while the rest of the family had one or at most two knives among them. The very well-to-do might own, as a matter of great pride, a few pewter dishes and spoons; but these were unusual. There were always a few iron cooking kettles. Beyond that the necessities and luxuries of life were to be fashioned in the wilderness from the original materials.

The journey began propitiously under the direction of the Boones. Squire had been over the road so often that he knew it every foot, where the best camping places were, and how long each day's journey should be. All went well until they were well into the mountains and were actually approaching the gap.

Here the party went into camp to await the arrival of still others who had agreed to meet them at this point: some forty men who had decided to go without their families for the time being, and a man named Russell. While waiting Boone sent his eldest son, James, a boy of sixteen, with two men and some pack horses to notify Russell and to get some flour and farming tools that had been promised. They made the journey safely, and were returning laden, accompanied by Russell's son, two of Russell's negro slaves, and two or three white workmen. Somehow they either missed their way, or were belated, and went into camp for the night only about three miles from the main party. At daybreak they were fired into by a Shawnee war party and all were killed on the spot except one of the white labourers and a negro, who managed to escape. Boone hearing the firing galloped up with his men; but too late.

This tragedy not only threw the little party into the profoundest grief for those who had been killed, but it also gave pause to the whole enterprise. There had been no expectation of Indian hostility on this side of the mountains. This might be merely a chance raiding party of a few irresponsible braves, of course; but, on the other hand, it might be intended as a warning that immigration of settlers would not be tolerated. Indians were no fools. Except in moments of drunkenness or ungovernable anger, they always treated well the traders, of whatever nationality, who came among them. Often, as we have seen, they even half tolerated the stray hunters who pushed out in advance of exploration. But on settlement they were apt to look with suspicion, or even with hostility.

It must be remembered that this venture was a little different from any of the pioneering that had gone before. Heretofore the frontier had been extended by somebody's going to live just a little farther out than anybody else, but still keeping in touch. It was a slow growth outward. But here these settlers were pushing boldly out to form an island entirely surrounded by savagery.

So these few men thought that if the Indians had made up their minds to resist, it would be mad folly to cut themselves away from all support. What could forty do against thousands? In spite of Boone's protests it was decided to abandon the expedition. They were not cowards, lightly turned aside by the first opposition, but they considered the time not propitious.

Some of them returned to whence they had come; but the majority, Boone among them, having sold their old farms, were unwilling to turn back. So they settled in the Clinch Valley, near where they had stopped, and there made themselves homes.

CHAPTER VIII

WE ARE now in our story face to face with the Indians, as was Boone. Perhaps it might be well to say a few words about them, so that we can have a clearer idea of the long series of fights that are now to follow.

There are two schools of opinion about the Indian, as there are two schools about the accuracy of the flint-lock rifle: and, as in that case, the truth lies somewhere between them. One school paints him as a fiend incarnate, without a single redeeming feature, a wild beast. That, it must be confessed, was the view held by perhaps a majority of the borderers. The other school depicts him as the "noble redman" possessed of all the primitive virtues; despoiled of his ancient heritage; cheated and robbed and made vicious by the injustice of the whites; a lofty and pathetic figure. There is truth in both pictures: and there is falsity.

You must remember, to start with, that the Indians of those days must not be judged by the Indians we know now. They were of a different and in many respects higher stock than the plains Indians we are most apt to see. In addition, they were living their own life in their own country, and so possessed faculties in full exercise. In a hundred and fifty years of a different kind of existence the Indian will change mentally and physically as fast as, or faster than, the white, and we all know the difference even two generations will make in our foreign immigrants. So first of all, consider the Indian of Boone's time as a very intelligent person, with a high sense of tradition, living a life that was fitted to him, and therefore developing to a high point of his capabilities. Since he had to make his own living and protect himself he was keen and sharp intellectually; so that his great men were indeed great men with judgment well developed. There were certain ideals he held to very rigidly. He had a high sense of his personal integrity, so that he would rather die—and often did—than smirch his honour in any way. Of course his idea of what was honourable might differ in some respects from ours, but such as it was he held to it a lot more consistently than we are apt to do, and would sacrifice to it more unhesitatingly than most of us. Also it must be confessed that most of his points of honour were ad- mirable—courage, endurance of pain, generosity, loyalty to friendship, faithfulness to a trust once undertaken are all

STRUGGLE

pretty good qualities. They are not bad ideals for us to uphold.

Nobody ever really doubted an Indian's courage, though it was customary to speak of the "cowardly skulking savage." It was part of the settled system of tactics in Indian warfare never to suffer undue loss. War to them meant inflicting loss on the other fellow, not the winning of what we call victory. With practically an unbroken forest between the Atlantic Coast and the Mississippi River it could not seem vastly important to them whether they held or gained any certain point in that forest or not. But in hand-to-hand combat or in the higher courage that barehanded meets danger unruffled the Indian must command respect. With us a coward is looked down upon; among those Indians he was quite apt to be eliminated. The celebrated chief Cornstalk is said to have tomahawked those of his own men who showed the slightest signs of flinching.

The endurance of pain, and incidentally of discomfort, was with them a religion. Early in life the children were practised in hardships. At eight years a child was made to fast a half day at a time; at twelve a whole day; at eighteen he was placed in a camp some miles from his village and fasted as long as he could hold out without absolutely perishing. When he had stood all of that he could, he was plunged into cold water. This was by way of practice. It was a point of honour never to show signs of suffering, so that people began to think Indians actually did not suffer; but their nervous systems were much the same as ours.

When captured the tortures became a contest between the enemies: one to elicit some sign of pain, and the other to endure. It is many times on record that a captive, while undergoing tortures so exquisite that it is useless to harrow your imaginations with an account of them, nevertheless laughed at his captors, reviling them as rank amateurs, and informing them that if any of them ever got caught by his tribe they would learn how to do it. One young man, after some hours of torment, informed his tormentors that if they would bring him certain materials he would show them some tortures worth while. They did so; and he demonstrated on his own body!

In their generosity they were whole hearted. It was literally a fact that they "shared their last crust," not once and as a special deed of beneficence, but always and as a matter of course. If a visitor in any of their villages happened to enter one of their dwellings, he was at once offered food, the best that dwelling possessed. To refuse it or not to offer it was equally insulting. This was done even though the house might be literally starving and the visitor fresh from a banquet. On the march also the proverbial "last crust" was always shared. The testimony of captives, otherwise roughly treated, is that their captors divided scrupulously the scanty provisions and that the prisoners always received their full shares. Colonel James Smith, who was captured by the Delawares, tells of this: "If any of the town folks would go to the same house several times in one day," he writes, "he would be invited to eat of the best; and with them it is bad manners to refuse to eat when it is offered.   At this time hominy, plentifully mixed with bear's oil and sugar, or dried venison, bear's oil, and sugar is what they offer to everyone who comes in any time of the day; and so they go on until their sugar, bear's oil, and venison are all gone, and then they have to eat hominy by itself without bread, salt, or anything else; yet still they invite everyone that comes in to eat while they have anything; but if they can in truth only say we have got nothing to eat, this is accepted as an honourable apology."   Another incident narrated by Smith gives an excellent example of how seriously this type of Indian took his obligations.   He was on an expedition with his friend, Tontileaugo; himself with a horse, the Indian with a canoe.   On account of a high wind they encamped for some days near the shore of a lake.   Tontileaugo went to hunt, leaving Smith to keep camp.   "When he was gone," Smith records, "a Wyandot came to our camp.   I gave him a shoulder of venison which I had by the fire well roasted, and he received it gladly: told me he was hungry, and thanked me for my kindness. When Tontileaugo came home I told him that a Wyandot had been at camp, and that I gave him a shoulder of roasted venison. He said that was very well, 'and I suppose you gave him also sugar and bear's oil to eat with his venison.'   I told him I did not as the sugar and bear's oil were down in the canoe, I did not go for it.   He replied, 'You have behaved just like a Dutchman.   Do you not know that when strangers come to our camp we ought always to give them the best we have?' I acknowledged that I was wrong. He said that he could excuse this, as I was but young: but I must learn to behave like a warrior, and do great things."

Loyalty was another of their virtues that was developed consistently to a very high point. The books are full of stories wherein an Indian friend of a white man has undergone great difficulty and danger to carry warning or safety to his pal among the whites. There have even been instances where the carrying of that warning meant certain death. As to faithfulness to the given word, that is a trait of the wild Indians to this day. Twenty-odd years ago, in the Hudson Bay country, I found that the post keepers were accustomed to extend credit for all sorts of supplies to quite large amounts. The Indians would then disappear into the forest and be lost to view for a year. I asked the Factor whether he did not lose considerable sums by this loose way of doing business; but he assured me that in all his experience he had known of but one Indian defaulter. Sometimes in a bad season the Indian might not come back the next year, but sooner or later he returned and paid his debt.

The Indians also held strictly to their treaties as far as they were able to do so. There were always two factors working against any complete carrying out of tribal as contrasted with personal agreements: one was drink, and the other was the fact that the authority of the chiefs who made the agreements was limited. It was literally true that at times they "could not control their young men"; and it is literally true that each warrior thought of himself first as an independent individual and only second as a responsible member of a community. The chiefs might make a peace which all would observe except a few headstrong young men; but a raid by those few was quite enough. Again the chiefs might promise safe-conduct to the inhabitants of a fort surrendering, but in some fashion the Indians might get access to rum and a massacre would follow. For more than any other human creature liquor seems to change the Indian. He is totally insane when drunk.

So well did they themselves know this that when serious deliberations were on they banished the rum pannikin. Their councils were formal, and they never made decisions until all sides were heard; and then not until twenty-four hours had passed for deliberation.

They were good tacticians in their own kind of warfare. Their movements were intelligent and wonderfully carried out, especially considering the thick cover and the difficulties of keeping in touch with each other. The various manœuvres were commanded by various sorts of whoops. Each man fought for himself his individual fight; and yet the sum total of all these individual fights was somehow handled as a unit. And they were very effective warriors. The white man in battle won a number of "victories," and suffered some crushing defeats, but many of the victories were at heavy cost and because, as we have seen, the Indian measured success not by ground gained or held, but by loss inflicted. It is not generally known that at every battle of any importance except that of Point Pleasant the whites greatly outnumbered the Indians. This was especially true at what have been called decisive battles—Bushy Run where Bonquet by clever strategy gained the day, but over inferior numbers, and only after a bitter struggle wherein he lost four times as many men; or Anthony Wayne's final engagement, where he outnumbered the Indians three to one. The losses were nearly always correspondingly disproportionate. Braddock's and Grant's regulars, without knowledge of Indian warfare, are estimated to have slain about one Indian for every hundred of themselves who fell! Naturally when the whites were skilled backwoodsmen this proportion fell off; but rarely—in spite of boastful accounts of the participants—were losses equal. Roosevelt says in his "Winning the West":

"In Braddock's war the borderers are estimated to have suffered a loss of fifty souls for every Indian slain; in Pontiac's war they had learned to defend themselves better and the ratio was probably as ten to one; whereas in this war, if we consider only males of fighting age, it is probable that a good deal more than half as many Indians as whites were killed." This was because of two things: the white man hated to run away in any circumstances, while the Indian would just as soon run away as not if there was anything to be gained by it; and the average white man could never quite equal the average Indian in woodcraft. Boone and such men as Kenton, Wetzel, Brady, McCulloch, and Mansker, could beat the Indian at his own game; but they were the exceptions. We will tell more about that when we get to the great wars. At present we are merely illustrating Indian intelligence and effectiveness in their sort of contest.

But there were four major traits in the otherwise most admirable and human character of the redman, and a number of minor faults that made all the trouble.

The major traits were cruelty, love of liquor, a capacity for hatred and revenge that equalled their capacity for friendship and loyalty, and improvidence. Their minor faults were an inability to do long-continued team work, a touchy pride, ungovernable rages.

Cruelty was partly born in them and partly the result of the training in bearing hardship and pain. If you have schooled yourself to pay no attention to a cut finger you have little patience with the fellow who bellows and raises a big fuss over it. Extend that idea and you will see what I mean. The fact remains that the Indian was inconceivably cruel, not only to his enemies, but to his domestic animals. Children were from the earliest years present at the tortures and taught to take part in them. It was part of a warrior's education. Like all children everywhere they carried over this business of life into their play. They played prisoner; they played torture; and often they used some unfortunate animal as a toy to give reality to the game. The result was inevitable: a cruelty for cruelty's sake that has been equalled only by the Holy Inquisition of the Middle Ages. Roosevelt says:

"Any one who has ever been in an encampment of wild Indians, and has had the misfortune to witness the delight the children take in torturing little animals will admit that the Indian's love of cruelty for cruelty's sake cannot possibly be exaggerated. The young are so trained that when old they shall find their keenest pleasure in inflicting pain in its most appalling form. Among the most brutal white borderers a man would be instantly lynched if he practised on any creature the fiendish torture which in an Indian camp either attracts no notice at all, or else excites merely laughter."

Thus cruelty became, you must remember, not a result of individual evil-mindedness or malice. When an Indian was cruel it was rarely in the personally malevolent fashion of a small boy tin-canning a dog: but it was because that was one of his racial characteristics. Outside his rages and enemies, or those who might become enemies, he was particularly warm-hearted. We have seen examples of his generosity and loyalty. In his tribal relations he was a merry and warm-hearted person. He rarely whipped his children, of whom he was very fond. If they must be punished he did it by ducking them under water. Colonel Smith, in mentioning this, remarks quaintly: "As might be expected, their children are more obedient in winter than in summer!" Nevertheless, a deep ingrained racial cruelty is one of the Indian characteristics; and was a powerful factor, when the scales of Eternal Justice were poised, in bringing about his elimination from the land. For however little it may be any one person's fault, if fault there be, it must have its consequence. To demonstrate responsibility by examples, both great and small, is possibly one reason our world exists.

An amazing illustration of this complete indifference to the other fellow's feelings in the matter is supplied by a contemporary account of a captivity among the Delawares. This man's companions were killed from ambush and he was seized.

"They then set off and ran at a smart pace for about fifteen miles, and that night we slept without fire. The next morning they divided the last of their provisions and gave me an equal share, which was about two or three ounces of mouldy biscuit: this and a young ground hog, about as large as a rabbit, roasted, and also equally divided, was all the provision we had until we came to the Loyal Hamm, which was about fifty miles." On arrival at the Indian village, however, the Indians ran out in great numbers "stripped naked, excepting breech clouts, and painted in the most hideous manner, of various colours. As they approached, they formed themselves into two long ranks. I was told by an Indian that could speak English that I must run betwixt these ranks and that they would flog me all the way as I ran. I started to the race with all the resolution and vigour I was capable of exerting, found that it was as I had been told, for I was flogged the whole way. When I got near the end of the lines I was struck with something that appeared to me a stick, or the handle of a tomahawk, which caused me to fall to the ground. On my recovering my senses I endeavoured to renew my race; but as I arose someone cast sand in my eyes, which blinded me so I could not see where to run. They continued beating me most intolerably, until I was at length insensible; but before I lost my senses I remember my wishing them to strike the fatal blow for I thought they intended killing me."

The Indians then took him to Fort DuQuesne and put him under the care of a French surgeon. It took him some time to recover; then the Indians reclaimed him and ever after, for the four years of his captivity, treated him with the greatest affection, as one of themselves. Our hero enquired of the Indian who spoke English, "a man of considerable understanding. I asked him if I had done anything that had offended the Indians, which caused them to treat me so unmercifully. He said no; it was only an old custom the Indians had, and that it was like 'how do you do.' "

When this innate and everyday and thoughtless cruelty was carried into border warfare and used by the savages against men, women, and children indiscriminately, it aroused a vindictive hatred and thirst for revenge that had behind it a strong driving force. Of that more later.

The second great fault, that of drunkenness, was the first cause of the Indian's undoing. In the old phrase, "he could not carry his liquor well." Indeed rum made of him a different man, an irresponsible, insane creature who was likely to do almost anything. The Indians recognized this themselves. Many travellers and traders describe to us the orderly fashion in which the savages used to arrange for a big drunk; depositing all their arms in a safe place; detailing certain members of the band whose duty it was to keep sober for the purpose of preventing deadly fights, to take care of the helplessly intoxicated, and to see that none of the maddened participants managed to get hold of weapons. When all these matters were arranged, the lucky ones who had the privilege proceeded deliberately to get drunk. These sprees were terrible, lasting sometimes two or three days; and it was a rare thing that, in spite of those delegated to stay sober, someone was not badly injured or killed. All the savage passions seemed to be unleashed by the liquor. They shrieked and yelled and danced and rolled on the ground; they staggered away aimlessly, and woe to the man who stood in their way! The great massacres, as at Fort William Henry, were not due to any prearranged plan—quite the contrary—but to the fact that the savages, armed, got access to the liquor barrels. The Indians themselves realized thoroughly all these facts. One of the traders testifies of them that they were "reasonable when sobered, and do not bear a grudge for violence by traders to subdue them when drunk." At the little trading outposts a supply of laudanum was always on hand to be mixed with the rum when matters were going too far. We shall add that the Indian soon grew to love alcohol with a great longing, so that he would travel great distances and part with anything to get it. No negotiation or purchase or sale had any chance of success unless the rum pannikin was forthcoming or promised.

Every settler's cabin in those days had its whiskey jug; every fort its supply of liquor. Such things were a matter of course, a daily supply, a ration as habitual as bread. So in a successful raid the savages always found the wherewith to inflame his mind; and thus by the light of burning cabins atrocities were committed beyond what even native cruelty would have urged without the liquor. And that added to the trouble. If you had laboured for some years hard, with axe and plough, and had at length bit by bit made yourself a cabin and a little farm; if one by one you had accumulated and bred until you had a tiny little herd of cows and pigs; if you and your wife had worked early and late, and your little baby was just getting big enough to toddle to the door to meet you—and then suppose some evening at sundown you were to return home from an absence, full of eagerness, and as you came around the point of the woods you saw a blackened smoking heap where your cabin had stood. As you ran forward you saw your cattle killed and left wantonly where they had fallen; your crops burned down. And at the house lay your little baby, its skull crushed when some Indian swung it by the feet against a tree. Your wife was gone. In desperation you aroused the neighbours, and perhaps by fortune you overtook the Indians after a number of days' travel. The Indians had had time to torture her. Your gentle, pretty wife has had her nails bent back; she has had her soft body burned by gun barrels heated red hot; she has had charges of powder fired into her; she has had the joints of her ten fingers and

her ten toes burned off one by one. She has in her prolonged agony cried for water, and they have brought her
molten lead. Perhaps I should not tell you even these few
details, but it is necessary for you to get the vivid picture
so you can gain even a faint understanding. Purposely I
have omitted the worst of the Indian tortures. They were
expert at prolonging the most exquisite agony for a very
long period. One man writing at the time said that the
"Indians could *only* torture him *three hours* before he died;
but his screams were particularly horrible." I quote from
memory. Can you wonder that such a man whose place
you have for the moment taken, and all his neighbours,
looked on the perpetrators of such a tragedy as fiends? And
when this, or worse, happens not once or twice, but hundreds of times, can you marvel that at last the tendency was
for the average settler to look on *all* Indians as wild beasts
to be shot at sight as wild beasts are?

And you must remember that the Indian was kind, generous, and loyal to those who were his friends, or against
whom he did not make war. Only, he made war cruelly;
and so in the slow movement of evolution he had to take the
consequences.

This antagonism between white and red was further in-
tensified by the Indian's fierce and haughty pride. He was
very touchy. Inclined to be friendly at first, he was in-
flamed to sudden anger at fancied slights or rebuffs. Very
tender of his dignity was he; and very suspicious that his
dignity was of set purpose assailed. Once he had a griev-

ance, or thought he had, he was revengeful to an extraordinary degree.   Things a white man would never notice, or if he did notice, would forget the next instant, the Indian would brood over and make a reason for retaliation.   And that retaliation might come instantly, in a burst of rage; or it might not come about until years later.   If possible it was at once, for the savage was subject to fits of ungovernable anger.   It is very hard, at the best, to get along with such people.   We all have them among our acquaintance, and they take very careful handling.   But the white borderers were not inclined to be particularly tender of their red neighbours' feelings; looking down on them as savages, and treating them with at best a good-natured tolerance and at worst with a fierce contempt.   Each side thus firmly believed itself superior to the other: for the Indian considered himself in every way better than the white—in honour, in bravery, in military skill, in endurance, in woodcraft. As to all but the first, they were certainly right, and as to honour, within their understanding of that term, they held to their code at least as closely as we did to ours.   They did not understand our virtues of steadfastness, industry, inventiveness, and the like.

"The Indians do not fear our numbers, which they deride," writes Eastburn, "because of our unhappy divisions in consequence of which they expect to conquer us completely."

Thus just in the make-up of the two races we have good

material for trouble; even if nothing else were to urge them against each other.

But the last of the evil fairies of the Indian disposition was his improvidence. He had little or no notion either of producing enough of anything to assure the future, or of saving a little to-day so as to have something for to-morrow. Most of us are a bit unwise that way; but the germ of thrift is in our race, and it was not in the Indian. We have seen how he fed everybody who entered his dwelling until the last was gone, even with a hard winter ahead and though the visitor had just had eight square meals. That was exactly typical. He raised some corn and vegetables, to be sure, because he liked them; but he rarely made sufficient store to last him through the season: and the winters were histories of famines.

This trait was not entirely, nor even principally, ignoble. It sprang not so much from laziness as from faith. The Indian, within his simple belief, was deeply religious, in that he made his religion a part of his daily life. He believed that death did not amount to very much, that men went right on doing things on the other side of the Veil, and that to pass from this life to that was merely like going from a forest he knew to one he did not know. Indeed the usual way of expressing death in some tribes was to say that a man "changed his climate." One of the beliefs of his religion was that men are under the personal care of the Great Spirit; that nothing can happen to them without the consent and intention of the Great Spirit; that good luck and bad luck, fortune and misfortune, happiness and misery, plenty and famine, are all bestowed by the Great Spirit for the purpose of punishing, rewarding, training, or developing his children.

Our old friend, James Smith, after he had been for a long time captive of the Delawares, was out with an old Indian named Tecaughutanego and a little boy named Nunganey. They were forty miles from anywhere, and they had the bad luck to encounter a spell of weather that made so thick a snow crust that Smith could not kill meat. The old man was laid up with rheumatism. After a while things, to Smith, became desperate. It looked as though nothing could save them from starvation. For two days he had had nothing at all to eat, and had hunted frantically. The old Indian and the boy had huddled at home in the hut trying to keep warm and conserve their strength. But let Smith tell about it:

"When I came into our hut Tecaughutanego asked what success. I told him not any. He asked me if I was not very hungry. I replied that the keen edge of appetite seemed to be in some measure removed, but I was both faint and weary. He commanded Nunganey to bring me something to eat, and he brought me a kettle with some bones and broth."

This was made, it seemed, from some old bones of fox and wildcat that the ravens and buzzards had left. They did not contain much substance, but they warmed and revived Smith. Then the old Indian filled and lighted his pipe, and handed it to his white friend, waiting patiently until it was smoked out. After Smith, in answer to his inquiries, stated himself much refreshed, the old man said that he had something of importance to communicate.

"He said the reason he deferred his speech till now was that few men are in a right humour to hear good talk when they are extremely hungry, as they are then generally fretful and discomposed; 'but as you now appear to enjoy calmness and serenity of mind, I will now communicate to you the thoughts of my heart, and those things I know to be true.

" 'Brother: as you have lived with the white people, you have not had the same advantage of knowing that the Great Being above feeds his people, and gives them their meat in due season, as we Indians have who are frequently out of provisions, and yet are wonderfully supplied, and that so frequently that it is evidently the hand of the great Owaneeyo that does this. Whereas the white people have commonly large stocks of tame cattle that they can kill when they please, and also their barn cribs filled with grain, and therefore have not the same opportunity of seeing and knowing that they are supported by the Ruler of heaven and earth.

" 'Brother: I know that you are now afraid that we will all perish with hunger, but you have no just reason to fear this.

" 'Brother: I have been young, but now am old; and I have frequently been under the like circumstances that we now are, and that some time or other in almost every year of my life; yet I have hitherto been supported, and my wants supplied in times of need.

" 'Brother: Owaneeyo sometimes suffers us to be in want, in order to teach us our dependence upon him, and to let us know that we are to love and serve him; and likewise to know the worth of the favours we receive and make us thankful.

" 'Brother: Be assured that you will be supplied with food, and that just in the right time; but you must continue diligent in the use of means. Go to sleep, and rise early in the morning and go a-hunting; be strong, and exert yourself like a man, and the Great Spirit will direct your way.' "

It is pleasant to relate that the old man's words were justified, and that the very next day Smith ran across some buffalo and managed to kill a cow.

But such faith in divine care naturally takes it for granted that the means must be at hand. These Indians had no belief in manna from heaven. They thought Owaneeyo would throw game in their way when it suited his purpose: but there must be game to throw. If a race of men are to depend solely on the natural sustenance of the wilderness, then they need a very large area of country. Wild animals require more space than tame and pasture-fed animals; so do wild men. The Indians realized very thoroughly that the coming of the white man in any numbers portended the killing and driving away of the game: which meant in time that the Great Spirit could no longer take care of his children. So the wars were not only wars of revenge, wars of hatred, but were also wars of preservation of what they considered their own, wars to defend the very continuance of the kind of life in agreement with their religion.

CHAPTER IX

NOR as a race were the white men without blame. Never did the most brutal of them quite get down to the ferocious cruelty of the Indians; but it must be remembered that cruelty with the Indians was something taught as honourable against an enemy, while with the white man it was purely a personal matter. Nevertheless, some of them were bad enough; and we seem to have had an unhappy faculty of doing things that alienated even those inclined at first to be friendly.

The pioneers were a rough race, even with each other. They were moulded for a hard job; and with the majority of them fineness of fibre or delicacy of feeling was not marked. Their jokes were boisterous and crude, their manners noisy; their perceptions quite incapable of appreciating the fact that they might be hurting the other man's feelings. In their every-day dealings they had little of that grave and calm ceremony so much esteemed by the Indians. Add to these natural disadvantages the fact that they looked down on the savages with contempt which they took small pains to conceal; and you can readily see that there could be no great sympathy between the races.

But we must go a step beyond that. There is no doubt but that the white man committed many unwarranted deeds of aggression. One of the worst was his persistence in selling the Indians liquor. We have seen how rum changed the savage's whole nature. The earliest settlers soon realized that with the help of a little fire water the Indian could be persuaded to almost anything. It was very useful in making treaties or trading. By its aid thousands of bad bargains—for the red man—were carried through quite legally; bargains great and small, but ending always in the Indian having less than he had before. It was all open and above board; and the savage went into it of his own free will; but the fact remained that his judgment had been clouded, or completely taken away. When he came to himself, he realized this fact. He could not do anything about it, but, dimly or clearly, he felt the injustice and nursed a grievance. And on the next occasion the same thing happened again; for once he had acquired the taste, he could not resist. Many of the greater chiefs knew this, and begged the whites to keep liquor from their people. It might be stated in justice to the whites that whiskey and rum were with them part of every bargain, business transaction, or social gathering. Even church business was carried forward with vast seas of port and madeira. It was considered no disgrace to get drunk: indeed that was quite as natural a way of enjoying oneself as is now a game of cards or dancing. A sot was looked down on simply because he allowed pleasure to elbow aside the other business of life. So our ancestors probably did not even have a passing suspicion that they were doing anything immoral in thus furnishing liquor. As to the cheating, as we would now call it, that was an age of individualism, wherein every man was supposed to take care of himself. We, in these days of the team-work idea, find it difficult to realize how completely this was true. Every man was responsible only to himself for ninety-nine hundredth of his actions. Unless these actions directly and immediately harmed his neighbours, he could do as he pleased. He might wantonly kill a perfectly friendly Indian on the very fringe of town; his action might be deplored or even frowned upon by his neighbours, but he would not be called to account. I am writing of borderers, not of the early blue-law Puritans. The neighbours would stop him fast enough if he tried to steal something off the wall, because they could see where that affected them: but so strongly were they independent as individuals that they could not perceive that in the long run Indian killing affected them more. And so we see the first racial uneasiness begin to smoulder from a feeling of injustice.

And a feeling of injustice in the matter of lands and pelts was strengthened by individual injustices of all kinds. There were three widely divergent classes of people who inflicted them: the strictly religious, the irresponsible ruffians, and those whose deadly enmity had been aroused by border outrages.

The first sort is very well illustrated by the performance of that sweetly tolerant lot we revere as the Puritans. They were at first very well received by the Indians. One warrior in especial took a great liking to them, and was constantly with them and doing all sorts of favours for them. When the first Thanksgiving was proclaimed, he hastened to the forest eager to supply his bit to the white man's feast, and had the luck to kill a fat buck. He carried the deer on his shoulders to the settlement and proudly presented it to his new friends. They had him whipped. Why? Because he had killed the deer on Sunday! What did the poor, friendly, eager savage know of Sunday? And what possible difference could it make to any but the religiously insane when a kind and generous deed is done! But you can imagine that the poor Indian, sore, bewildered, changed his mind about being a friend of the white man; and changed the minds of his people as far as his influence extended. There were many similar instances.

The ruffians were an even more serious matter. You must realize that a good many of the more southerly settlers were actually convicts, either sent over from the old country to be got rid of, or brought in as bondsmen. They and their descendants could not be expected to exemplify all the virtues. And among the better element are always roughs, men without scruple, scornful of the other man's rights, overbearing, bullying, ready fighters, indifferent to consequences, hard drinkers, "tough" boys.   These are hard enough to handle in a modern city with all the facilities of a police system.   It was absolutely impossible to handle them in those days of individual irresponsibility, and nobody tried.   They committed all sorts of absolutely unprovoked outrages; and the hatreds and revenges they inspired were laid to the whole white race.   That sort of thing was done by both sides.   A white settler who had lost family or friends was thenceforth an enemy of the Indians, good or bad; an Indian who had been insulted or cheated or maltreated by some renegade killed the first white man he saw. There was little to choose between the two sides; and these things, from small beginnings, accumulated, became worse and worse, until there was an abiding enmity.   The wonder is not that white men and red men were so merciless to each other, but rather that there persisted so much personal friendship and mercy and decency in spite of everything.

But outside of any question of justice or injustice, we must not forget that nothing could have saved the Indian in his old manner of life.   He occupied and owned vast areas of land in the sense that he roamed over it and killed game on it.   In the broader sense of ever having done anything to make it useful or productive he did not occupy it nor own it at all.   Whether by peace or war, whether by slow evolution or swift force, it has always been the history of the world that nomadic peoples disappear before pastoral peoples, and they in turn give way to agricultural peoples. Sometimes the same race develops from hunters to herdsmen to farmers: sometimes, as with the Indian and with the Californian-Spanish, it is thrust aside. As the country became settled, as it was necessary that fewer acres be required to support more people, it would be inevitable either that the Indian move on to a fresh game country or that he modify his nomadic life and support himself in a new way. That is a law of evolution, and cannot be avoided.

And in the present instance the Indians had less than their usual shadow of a title to the land. The country south of the Ohio was a debatable ground always. It lay between the Cherokee races on the south and the Algonquin races on the north, and was used by both as a hunting and battle ground, but was settled by neither. Daniel Boone and his companions, members of a third race, going into Kentucky for the same purposes, thereby acquired just as good a title. However, as will be seen, treaties were here also made and broken.

There we are. After some centuries of contact the two races, rightly or wrongly, faced each other as enemies.

The Indians were formidable fighters; and in those days had advantages denied our plains Indians in their period of warfare with the whites. It is easier to learn plains' craft or mountain craft than woodcraft. Two or three men in the mountains or on the prairie can stand off a great number of Indians. But these savages dwelt and travelled and fought in a region of dark, tangled, gloomy forests. It was a forest of dense leafy undergrowth so thick that one could rarely see more than a few yards, and yet so yielding that one could glide almost anywhere through it. The high, straight trunks of the trees rose above it, branching and forked, leaning, the most excellent observation posts where a warrior could sit at ease scanning the mobile sea of brush beneath. No horse could travel through it except on chopped paths or game trails, so that it was easy for the ambuscading savage to guess his mounted foe's route. Indeed even a foot traveller—unless he was an expert in woodcraft beyond the skill of most people even in those days—who strayed a hundred yards off known routes would be hopelessly lost. In such a forest there are few landmarks, a terrifying similarity. Only very occasionally was this forest opened by a meadow in a valley, or a "park" on a hillside, but ordinarily one could travel literally for weeks on end without either seeing clearly the sun or any other prospect but the tree trunks and the thick, leafy screen of the underbrush. About the only exceptions were the "openings" in Kentucky.

Now it is all very well to have told you of the woodcraft education our little white boys were given, and it was a wonderful education; but it could not possibly equal that of the Indian lads. The red boy had the advantage of inheriting qualities the white boy's ancestry could not hand down to him; and in addition he was, in all this, leading his

IN THIS PATHLESS FOREST

normal every-day life, where the white boy was merely being taught, however thoroughly, for an emergency. As Roosevelt says:

"To their keen eyes, trained for generations to more than a wild beast's watchfulness, the wilderness was an open book; nothing at rest or in motion escaped them. They had begun to track game as soon as they could walk; a scrape on a tree trunk, a bruised leaf, a faint indentation of the soil which the eye of no white man could see, all told them a tale as plainly as if it had been shouted in their ear. They could no more get lost in a wilderness than a white man could get lost on a highway."

Their accustomed moccasins could move silently and surely among dried twigs and dead leaves. The "broken dried twig" of fiction has become somewhat of a joke, its mention occurs so often, yet any one who has done any still hunting in the forest knows that this is the most frequent, the most difficult to avoid, and the loudest and most advertising of any of the minor accidents. The ability to move with absolute silence is a rare gift. Savages shared it with cougars and wildcats.

And so in this pathless blinded forest, where every tree trunk, every leafy bush, every stone was a ready-made ambush, where thousands of obstacles to easy travel made the clumsy white man as obvious as a circus parade, the Indians moved, invisible, silent, watching their foes with fierce contempt, awaiting the moment to strike. For days they would follow a party as wolves follow a herd, skulking unsuspected, leaving a trail that only an expert could recognize.

They were never as good shots with the rifle as a white hunter; and as a rule they were not as strong physically in a rough-and-tumble; but they were better shots than the regular soldiers, and a hand-to-hand combat with knife and tomahawk they never avoided, and often won. They had superior endurance. Their ability to travel long distances enabled them to strike unexpectedly, and far from their own villages. They appeared silently from unknown forests, robbed and murdered, and disappeared. There was always the utmost difficulty in following them, and nobody could guess where next they would attack. Add to these things their cunning and quiet stealth, their courage and skill in fight, and the fiendish cruelty of their deeds, you cannot wonder that the settlers looked on them as devils out of the black forest.

Now can you longer wonder that when Braddock or Grant led into this wilderness the very best white troops trained in European warfare, they were not only defeated, but massacred? They were helpless. They could not stray thirty yards from the column without getting lost; and a column offered only too fair a mark to the savages. They could never catch the smallest glimpse of the silently flitting foe. The Indians attacked such clustered huddled opponents without the slightest hesitation, shooting them down as they would herded buffalo. The soldiers might as well have been blindfolded. It was only when the trained borderers took a hand that the white men made head, slowly. And now you can understand more clearly what it means when you are told that Boone, Kenton, Mansker, and their contemporaries beat the Indian at his own game.

CHAPTER X

WITH a full knowledge of the dangers and horrors of any determined Indian warfare before him, Daniel Boone knew better than to push forward into the new Paradise without some sort of backing; and as at present it seemed impossible to get that, he settled down in the Clinch Valley as patiently as he could to await the turn of events.

Now it happened that in those times, as to-day, it was the custom after a war was over to give the soldiers who had fought in that war a bounty or bonus. This took the form of lands. After the French war, that preceded the Revolution, the custom had been followed, and Virginia had located her bounty lands in Kentucky! To be sure nobody could get at that land; but, on the other hand, it was reported to be very rich, so it would probably be valuable some day. The legislators had no concern with ways and means. "Here," they told the soldiers, "the land is there:

for we have been reliably informed as to that fact. We have voted it to you. It is none of our business how you get it—or whether you ever get it."

But at that time a man named Lord Dunmore was Governor of Virginia. He was much hated and vilified later, when his loyalty to his own country impelled him quite naturally to take the British side, but he seems to have been a man of vision and of energy. He, too, was much taken with the stories of the new West; and in 1772 he had made arrangements to explore in company with George Washington. The expedition fell through, but both Washington—as a friend of the soldier; and Dunmore—as being interested in opening new country for his colony of Virginia—occupied themselves in making more definite the rather vague bounty claims. To this end they sent in surveyors.

These bold and hardy men under an expert woodsman named Thomas Bullitt, and including many names later famous, made their way down the Ohio River to the Falls; following thus the custom of taking the easy routes by waterway. Here they built a fortified camp and proceeded methodically about their business.

This was in 1773. The next year, as these were unmolested, other surveyors were sent in; and Captain James Harrod with a party of forty-one men came down the Ohio River looking out possible locations for the bounty land. Another party came up the Kentucky River to about the present site of Louisville. None of these men brought their families nor any of their household goods. They were exactly like the hunting parties who had preceded them, except that they had other thoughts in view besides the pursuit of game and pelts.

You may be sure the Indians viewed these encroachments with uneasiness. They had not yet come to the point of declaring an open war nor advancing on these rather strong bands of white men in sufficient force to destroy them; but raiding parties of young men were constantly on the war-path or on horse-stealing expeditions—a favourite form of sport. Lonely cabins on the east side of the mountains were attacked and their occupants killed or carried captive. Many white people were thus slain before a drop of Shawnee blood was shed. The borderers grew more and more exasperated and surly at these swift blows struck in the dark by an enemy who disappeared before the blow could be countered. Once in a while they set forth in retaliation, and then the chances were nine out of ten that they killed the wrong Indians, which made them still more enemies. Everything was ripe for a grand explosion. The whites were anxious for a war that would settle these forays; the Shawnees and Mingos were haughty and yet at the same time uneasy over the westward advance of the whites; Lord Dunmore desired to add definitely the Kentucky lands to his Colony of Virginia, and at the same time, probably, in view of the increasing trouble with England, he would have been delighted to distract the Virginians' minds by an Indian war. All that was needed was an excuse.

Lord Dunmore saw plainly that the excuse could not be

long wanting, and that if the surveying parties in the back country were not to perish in the first blast of the tempest, they must be immediately warned. In this need he sent for Daniel Boone, whose name was already well known, and whose daring journey was celebrated. As Boone expresses it, Lord Dunmore "solicited" him to go in to warn the surveyors.

"I immediately complied with the Governor's request," says Boone simply.

He picked out one of his acquaintance named Stoner, another master woodcraftsman, and the two started on their journey. It was doubly perilous, not only because of the growing hostility of the Indians, but also because the necessity of making speed rendered it impossible for them to be as careful as usual.

It was a most extraordinary feat, for it covered over eight hundred miles and was completed in two months. It was entirely overland, for the easier water routes—along which the surveyors had entered—were now closed by Indians. They found and visited all the surveyors' camps, no light feat in itself, and they warned Captain Harrod and his party of landlookers. Boone, with characteristic far-sightedness, lost no opportunity of getting more first-hand information of the land. So pressing was the need of this warning that only a few days after Boone's arrival at the Falls of the Ohio, while the surveyors and settlers were breaking camp getting ready to go, a number of them who had gone to the spring for water were attacked suddenly.

The survivors had to scatter and escape as best they could. One man, with the Indians about two jumps behind him, fled along an Indian trail and shortly arrived at the Ohio River. Here, at the end of the trail, by the greatest good luck, was a bark canoe. He flung himself into it and shoved off, lying low until the swift current at this part of the river had carried him out of range. By the time he dared raise his head he was far down stream, around many bends and headlands. To make head against the force of the stream, with probably the Indians waiting for him, seemed impossible; especially as the fugitive had no idea whether or not he would find his comrades still living. It seemed easier to keep on going, so he did. In the bark canoe he floated down the entire length of the Ohio and Mississippi rivers, a distance of two thousand miles, and in some manner made his way up the Atlantic coast to Philadelphia. It was certainly a roundabout way to get home, and a most extraordinary journey. The time was summer, so that wild grapes and berries were plentiful; besides which, like all frontiersmen who never stirred step without rifle, he was armed.

By secret ways and with great dangers and natural difficulties avoided Boone led his little band across the mountains and safe to civilization. The Hunter himself remarked that they overcame "many obstacles," which was an emphatic statement from him. Considering the fact that during his absence war had finally blazed in all its fury, so that now must be avoided an aroused and active foe,

Boone's successful conduct of this party was truly remarkable.

During his absence the needed spark had been struck that should fire the tinder so long prepared. At that time one of the most noted men on the border, red or white, was Logan, an Iroquois, but now chief among the Senecas and Mingos. He was a man of very high character, a great orator, a man of vision and intelligence, one who knew the integrity of his word and his honour. An individual named Lowden has told us that he considered "Logan the best specimen of humanity he ever met with either white or red," which is remarkable praise in that day when borderers like Lowden looked on "savages" with contempt. Logan was a noble specimen of a man, over six feet tall, straight as a pine tree, with an open and kindly expression. He had ever been the friend of the whites, using always all his influence for peace, and doing for them all the kindly deeds in his power. Especially was he a friend of children, noted for his gentleness to them. Nor was he less celebrated for his manly qualities. He was a good shot, and as mighty a hunter as Boone himself. Throughout the whole border he was liked by everybody, and treated by everybody with the greatest respect, for his manner was said to have been informed with a grave and lofty courtesy that seemed to exact an equal courtesy in return, even from the roughest men. It has been told of him that "he was greatly liked and respected by all the white hunters and frontiersmen whose friendship and respect were worth having: they admired him for his dexterity and prowess, and they loved him for his straightforward honesty and his noble loyalty to his friends."

Now just at this time three traders were attacked by some outlaw Cherokees, outlaw from even their own tribe; one was killed, one wounded, and their goods were stolen. Orders were issued by Lord Dunmore's lieutenant to the borderers to hold themselves in readiness to repel any attack by the Indians. On the strength of that, some of the reckless and lawless borderers started out to kill perfectly friendly and innocent Indians. And by what must seem always the most evil of all injustice, every member of Logan's family was most brutally murdered, nine in all, down to the last child. All these retaliatory killings fell on friendly Indians.

Immediately the flames of war blazed up. Swift runners loped through the forest carrying the news to distant tribes. The war poles were struck in many villages; and to the command of Cornstalk, the greatest of the war chiefs, came practically every warrior of four powerful tribes: the Shawnees, the Delawares, the Mingos, and the Wyandots. To the Indians, proud and warlike, and firmly convinced that they could conquer the whites and bar them from the country, the time seemed to have come for the supreme effort.

Logan did not wait for his own revenge. On learning of the slaughter of his family he gathered together a small band of Mingo warriors and fell on the settlement. He took there thirteen scalps. A party pursued; but he ambushed them cleverly, and defeated them, taking more scalps. Before the war had become general he made at least four of these bloody raids, perhaps more, burning, tomahawking, killing, and disappearing again as he had come. He was a wolf, sombre and terrible. Yet even in this paroxysm of grief, anger, and revenge his nobler qualities were not submerged. He was out to kill in his madness; yet when a prisoner was captured he refused to permit torture, and risked his own life to save the captive. A few days later he came to this white man bringing a quill, some paper, and ink made of gunpowder. Under dictation the prisoner wrote a short note addressed to Captain Cresap, whom Logan supposed to be the murderer of his family. This was a mistake. A trader named Greathouse had committed the deed. Then Logan made another raid, murdered the entire family of a white settler, and left the note tied to a war club. It read:

"Captain Cresap:

"What did you kill my people on Yellow Creek for? The white people killed my kin at Conestoga, a great while ago, and I thought nothing of that. But you killed my kin again at Yellow Creek, and took my cousin prisoner. Then I thought I must kill, too; and I have been three times to war since; but the Indians are not angry, only myself."

The great Seneca chief was wrong: the Indians were angry; and from the swarm that was gathering at Cornstalk's camp large bands detached themselves and fell upon the border. Terrible were the ravages. The settlers, gathered in the forts, could no longer hunt, could no longer cultivate their farms except at the deadly peril of their lives. Yet life must go on in spite of the danger. Houses were burned, crops destroyed, prisoners tortured. No one knew where a blow was to fall next. The forests were full of danger. Stealth and ferocity, as usual, characterized the forays. The marauders appeared out of a quiet peace before their proximity could be suspected, and disappeared as suddenly. They left no trail that could be successfully followed; nor, in the presence of the large bodies that now roamed the forests, was a pursuing party of a size any settlement could send out safe against being overwhelmed and massacred. And behind them they left a waste of charred timbers and of scalped and mangled corpses. Not in isolated places and occasionally were these scenes enacted, as heretofore; but anywhere, everywhere, at any time, so that from end to end the border was vocal with demoniac war whoops and shrieks of the victims, lurid with the glare of burning buildings and the rolling smokes of fires. In the dark woodlands were many desperate combats; for the whites, in a frenzy of anger so much the stronger as it was for the moment powerless, went forth in little bands seeking revenge. As the Indians were confident and full of the pride of success some of these woodland skirmishes were very deadly.

The border quailed before the fury of the storm, but it

did not break. Lord Dunmore realized that this was a
matter to be settled decisively not nibbled at; and like a
wise commander he was making adequate preparations.
These took time. By way of a diversion he advised the
frontiersmen to organize a raid on their own account, not
with the idea of conquering the Indians, but to keep them a
little busy. Four hundred of them gathered under Angus
McDonald, crossed the Ohio River a little over a hundred
miles below where Pittsburg stands, and marched to the
Muskingum River, in Ohio, where there were several
Shawnee towns. If you will look at the map, you will see
that this was sneaking in on them by way of the back door.
Most of the Shawnee warriors were away on other business.
The expedition had a smart fight with those who remained,
took five scalps—white men scalped as well as savages—
burned the villages, destroyed a lot of standing corn, and
returned. The Shawnees tried to ambush them on their
way home, but failed. The expedition was successful in
drawing off some of the warriors to defend their own
homes, and as a demonstration that the villages were not
quite as safe as they had thought. This was just about the
time Boone had reached the surveyors at the Falls.

While all this was going on Lord Dunmore was getting
what was for those days a really formidable army. It was
about three thousand strong. One wing of it was to be
under Dunmore himself. The other, composed entirely of
frontiersmen, was commanded by General Andrew Lewis.
The two wings were to march by separate routes and join

forces at the mouth of a river called the Great Kanawha, a stream that flowed into the Ohio River south of the most populous Indian villages. From there they would penetrate the Indian's country and give him a taste of his own medicine.

Matters were in this condition when Boone and Stoner returned with the surveyors. Boone at once proceeded to raise a company of riflemen and was about to march to join Lord Dunmore when he received instructions that in recognition of his services he had been commissioned as captain and had been given the very responsible job of commanding the frontier forts. While the expedition was on its way to bring terror to the Indian villages Boone must assure our own from counter-attack. He was very busy at it. So large a proportion of the men had gone to join Dunmore that Boone's garrisons were small, and had to be eked out with the boys and old men. Boone himself was continually passing stealthily from one to another, generally at night. His scouts were flung far out into the forest to give early warning of an attack. Instead of dividing and scattering his effective forces among the different forts, he trained a compact body of riflemen, and these he held ready always to move swiftly in aid when the outrunners brought news that any of the forts were attacked. In the military correspondence of that summer he is frequently mentioned in terms of the highest praise, even the usually scornful British officers speaking of him in "a respectful and even deferential tone." A contemporary writer tells of him as a familiar figure throughout the valley, as he hurried to and fro on his duties, "dressed in deerskin coloured black, and his hair plaited and clubbed up." There were alarms and attacks and short sieges in all of which the Scout's especial abilities came into better play than they would had he been merely one of Lord Dunmore's army.

Nevertheless, we can imagine his regret at not being with the main expedition, in spite of his well-known placidity of temper and philosophy of view.

In the meantime, something had occurred to change the original plan. You remember Lord Dunmore's section and General Lewis's section were to march by separate routes and meet at the junction of the Ohio and the Kanawha rivers. Suddenly Dunmore, who was at Fort Pitt with nineteen hundred of the total of three thousand men, decided that he would not join Lewis as planned, but instead floated down the Ohio in flatboats, built some log forts, and started on a raid of his own toward some Indian villages farther west. His troops were mainly Colonials, the most of the borderers being with Lewis; but he had under his command a number of famous scouts, among whom were George Rogers Clark, Cresap, and Simon Kenton. He managed to destroy a few towns, but the decisive engagement was denied him.

The other section under Lewis gathered at the Great Levels of Greenbriar, and was almost completely composed of backwoodsmen, "heroes of long rifle, tomahawk, and hunting shirt, gathering from every stockaded hamlet, every lonely clearing and smoky hunter's camp. They were not uniformed, save that they all wore the garb of the frontier hunter; but most of them were armed with good rifles, and were skilful woodsmen." They were gathered on an errand that appealed to the very heart of them. For years and years they had been forced to live in the strain of perpetual watchfulness, never knowing where tragedy was going to strike next, each with terrible memories seared into his soul. They had been brought up in the shadows of stockades around which prowled the darker shadows of an enemy who struck unexpectedly and whose face was rarely seen. Nor were they able to strike back except in a feeble way. They could, and did, resist direct attack; they could in small bands follow, for a short distance, the retreating marauders; but that was all. Ever had they to return, their hearts burning with sullen anger, their souls bitter. Now at last they were to be gathered in sufficient numbers to do something. Eagerly they assembled at Great Levels. The difficulty was not to get enough men; but to keep enough back to defend the settlements.

These borderers were in many respects the most formidable fighters, but they had one serious fault: They were utterly undisciplined. To do anything really effective with a body of men, you *must* have teamwork. No matter whether or not the individual thinks his commander is stupid, incompetent, and a dodo, and that he could avoid all those obvious mistakes, he must follow implicitly that commander's orders. A very poor plan carried out well is better than a very good plan carried out badly. We all know that: but in those days when each man was a law to himself, when each man was accustomed not only to forming his own opinions but to acting on them without interference, the result was an unruly and turbulent gathering. The officers were obeyed just so far as their orders seemed reasonable to the individual fighter or to the extent that he had personal influence or popularity. If the frontiersman did not happen to like the way things were going, he often went home without further ado. If he thought he had a better idea than the one embodied in the orders given by one of his officers, he shouted it forth; and if enough of his companions thought so, too, why they did it, orders or no orders. This often brought about disaster, as we shall see when we come to the battle of Blue Licks.

In view of the discipline we have imposed on ourselves, because we know it to be the effective thing, the following account is interesting. Imagine nowadays a colonel being thus treated by a private! Twenty years in Leavenworth for him! The private was named Abraham Thomas, a borderer, aged eighteen; and Colonel McDonald, a British officer in command. Thomas wrote:

"While laying here, a violent storm through the night had wet our arms, and M'Donald ordered the men to discharge them in a hollow log, to deaden the report. My rifle would not go off, and I took the barrel out to unbreech it. In doing this I made some noise beating it with my tomahawk, on which M'Donald came toward me, swearing, with an uplifted cane, threatening to strike. I instantly arose on my feet, with the rifle barrel in my hand, and stood in an attitude of defense. We looked each other in the eyes for some time; at last he dropped his cane and walked off, while the whole troop set up a laugh, crying, 'The boy has scared the Colonel!' "

Another incident:

"During this battle one of the men, Jacob Newbold, saw the Colonel lying snug behind a tree." A perfectly proper proceeding in this sort of warfare. "It was immediately noised among the men, who were in high glee at the joke: one would cry out, 'Who got behind the log?' when a hundred voices would reply, 'The Colonel! the Colonel!' At this M'Donald became outrageous; I heard him inquire for the man who had raised the report, and threaten to punish him." This was reported to Newbold who "raising on his feet and going toward the Colonel, he declared he did see him slink behind the log during the battle; he gave his rifle to a man standing by, cut some hickories, and stood on the defense, at which the whole company roared with laughter." Twenty years in Leavenworth? Forty! But it is related of the Colonel that he merely "took himself off to another part of the line."

To make such a body effective you must either have a leader whose reputation and experience are such that even these rough, cocksure men will obey them—such as Clark or Boone—or else you must have a great welding emotion that brings them firmly together in a common cause.

In this case it was the common cause.

The Indians, of course, were well aware of this gathering, and they were making their preparations in all confidence. As we have said, they had every belief that they would eventually conquer the white man; and they based this belief on just the trait we have been discussing. The white man seemed to be unable to do any teamwork. Time and again the watchful chiefs had seen their opponents come to grief because of their dissensions. This was the first time the borderers had ever got together animated by a single strong purpose, and the arrogant redmen were as yet unaware of what that meant. It still seemed to them that by the old good tactics of defeating their enemy piecemeal they were again to win by the usual great slaughter. Indeed, the change of plan by which Lord Dunmore failed to join Lewis seemed to them another example of the same thing, and they hastened to take advantage.

The war chief was Cornstalk. He was as celebrated and as remarkable in his way as Logan, a man of great intelligence, high honour, widespread influence, and military capacity. He was one of the few Indians at this time far-sighted enough to realize the actual situation and to estimate the white man's powers. Nobody doubted Cornstalk's courage, nor his loyalty to his own people; so in spite of his continued and strong opposition to this war, when once it was decided on there was no question but that he would be its military leader. He was, indeed, a statesman of high order, a great orator, a far-sighted seer who only too plainly foresaw the doom of his people. In the councils he steadily set his advice against the war; but when it was decided by vote he exclaimed: "Then since you are resolved to fight, you shall fight. But if any warrior shall attempt to run away, I shall kill him with my own hand."

In the failure of Dunmore to join forces with Lewis he saw a chance to carry out his favourite tactics, to cut up his enemy in detail. As Lewis had with him only eleven hundred men, while the Earl commanded some nineteen hundred, Cornstalk resolved to attack the former. In doing so it is probable he made a mistake, for Lewis's men were nearly all border fighters, accustomed to forest warfare, while most of Lord Dunmore's army were from nearer the seaboard. At this sort of combat one of the former was worth three—or more—of the latter. On the other hand, he may have reasoned that Lewis was less likely to be prepared.

At any rate, Cornstalk, as prompt to execute as he was wise to plan, led his long "Indian files" of painted warriors rapidly across the country. He had with him somewhere about a thousand of the picked young men of various tribes, some from as far even as the Great Lakes. Thus it will be seen that even here he was outnumbered.

In the meantime, Lewis's army was on the march. It was, as we have said, composed almost entirely of backwoodsmen; officers and men dressed alike in the hunting costume, fringed shirts, fur caps or felt hats, moccasins, often leggings and breech clout. They were armed with their rifles, their tomahawks, and their knives with which they took scalps as eagerly as did the savages. Unlike the Indians, however, they did not travel merely with what they could carry on their backs. This was to be a long and decisive campaign; they did not intend to return home until they had finished the job; and so it is on record that they drove beef cattle and had hundreds of packhorses laden with flour and munitions. With men inexperienced, or partly experienced, in these dense forests, such an incumbrance would have offered fatal opportunities for surprise and massacre. Braddock's campaign is the classic example. But these men knew how. They marched in many single-file columns well separated, with scouts flung well out in front and on the flanks, with axe-men to clear a way for the animals. No matter from which side the Indians might attack, this arrangement would offer the thin, widely extended line most effective in forest fighting. They cut straight across the unbroken wilderness, making their route as they went. In about three weeks they had arrived at the upper waters of the Kanawha. Here they stopped a week to build canoes, of which they made twenty-seven. Part of the army then floated down stream while the remainder marched. Still another week later they came to the mouth of the river and camped on the point of land.

Here Cornstalk attacked them; and here took place one of the most desperate Indian battles in history, stubbornly fought out on a small space of ground, the lines alternately swaying back and forth as attacks gained or leaders fell.

"The fight," says Roosevelt, "was a succession of single combats, each man sheltering himself behind a stump, or rock, or tree trunk." The battle lines, while over a mile long, were drawn so closely together in the thick underbrush of the forest that never were they more than twenty yards apart. Again and again the individual foemen, having discharged their rifles, would leap on each other in deadly struggle with tomahawk and knife. The woods were filled with the noises of battle, the smack and clatter of the rifles, the wild yells and war whoops of the fighters, the cries of the badly wounded, and the jeers and taunts of the adversaries. To insult your enemy was as customary in those days as it was in the times of Homer. It is related that Colonel Field "was at the time behind a great tree, and was shot by two Indians on his right, while he was trying to get a shot at another on his left who was distracting his attention by mocking and jeering at him." And, "The Indians also called out to the Americans in broken English, taunting them, and asking them why their fifes were no longer whistling—for the fight was far too close to permit of any such music." And up through the straight trunks and leafy branches floated and eddied the white powder smoke.

The Indians were, it is the universal testimony, remarkably well handled. Their headmen walked up and down behind the lines, holding their warriors fast, exhorting them to close in, to aim carefully, to keep courage. And all day long the white men could hear Cornstalk's deep and resonant voice booming out the words: "Be strong!   Be strong!"

Manœuvres of tactics were promptly carried out. Against any other army in the world but just this one the Indians would undoubtedly have won another of their spectacular and bloody victories.   But these backwoodsmen were stubborn and skilful; they recked little for losses, and each man could care for himself.   And since in the long day's battle neither side broke, at the close of the afternoon the Indians slowly withdrew.

It had been a bloody, hard-fought battle.   On the white men were inflicted two hundred and fifteen casualties out of the eleven hundred engaged, a very severe loss.   The Indians suffered only about half as heavily, but they felt it more, for their numbers were fewer and they had no great reserve to depend on.   That night they slipped across the Ohio.   The Americans were far too exhausted to pursue them.   By the time they were prepared to follow up their advantages the Indians had already opened negotiations for peace with Lord Dunmore.

For outside the very severe loss in the battle, a much larger loss than the Indian tactics ordinarily permitted, the Indian morale had received a severe shock.   The redmen had heretofore been absolutely convinced that in any large operation they could, in the forest, whip twice their number of whites, and whip them so badly that the final result would be a rout and a massacre.   They were fully justified in their belief.   That's the way it had happened heretofore; and generally because of some asininity in the conduct of the whites so glaring that the Indian can be readily excused in his contempt. About the only time the Indians had met with anything like a reverse was at Bushy Run where Bonquet, even with a greatly superior force, was just about beaten when he was saved by a body of provincial rangers, and at that suffered four times the casualties he inflicted. But here they had met a nearly equal force of white men and, if not defeated, had failed to gain the victory, and had undergone a loss they could not afford. Their mercurial spirits dropped into the profoundest gloom. A day before, they had in the arrogance of self-confidence unreasonably seen the future in their hands; now as unreasonably they went to the other extreme.

Only Cornstalk, that grim old chief, was undaunted, still ready to fight it out. He had foreseen this result; he had been forced into the war against his judgment; but now he alone stood erect at the council fire gazing with lofty scorn at the circle of silent blanketed warriors, who stared at the ground and showed not one flicker of response to the great War Chief's stirring eloquence.

"What shall we do now?" demanded Cornstalk at last. "The Long Knives are coming. Shall we turn out and fight them?"

Silence.

"Shall we kill our squaws and children, and then fight until we are killed ourselves?" persisted the stern old warrior.

Still a dead silence.

Cornstalk suddenly strode forward and struck his tomahawk deeply into the war post.

"Since you will not fight, I will myself make peace," said he bitterly.

The Indians agreed to Lord Dunmore's terms. They were to surrender all white prisoners and stolen horses then in the tribes, to give up all claim to any of the land south of the Ohio River, and to furnish hostages. They were very humble, all but Cornstalk. He agreed to the conditions, but throughout all the meetings his manner was one of haughty defiance; and he addressed Lord Dunmore with fierce reproach and a fiery disdain that showed his total personal indifference to danger. It is said that: "The Virginians, who, like their Indian antagonists, prized skill in oratory only less than skill in warfare, were greatly impressed by the Chieftain's eloquence, by his command of words, his clear distinct voice, his peculiar emphasis, and his singularly grand and majestic yet graceful bearing; they afterwards said that his oratory fully equalled that of Patrick Henry."

Cornstalk, however, held honourably to his promises, and did his best to live up to the terms of peace. Indeed in that manner he met his death; for less than a year after the opening of the Revolutionary War he came in to the fort at Mt. Pleasant to tell the commandant that, while he was, as always, anxious to keep the peace, the Indians were headstrong, and were probably about to go to war. He warned the whites that, in spite of his sentiments, if they did so, he would of course have to be true to his race and side with them. He and his companions stayed on as a sort of hostage for the time being. During this period, says Dodge, "Cornstalk held frequent conversations with the officers and took pleasure in describing to them the geography of the West, then little known. One afternoon, while he was engaged in drawing on the floor a map of the Missouri Territory, its watercourses and mountains, a halloo was heard from the forest, which he recognized as the voice of his son, Ellinipsico, a young warrior, whose courage and address were almost as celebrated as his own." The son had become uneasy of his father's absence and had come in search of him.

The next day two white men went hunting from the fort, were waylaid and killed by some stray Indians. Their companions, hearing the shots, found the bodies, and at once, headed by their precious captain, a man named John Hall, rushed to the fort shouting: "Kill the red dogs in the fort!" The fort's other officers tried to intervene, but were swept aside. Cornstalk and his friends heard the cries, and recognized the situation.

"Do not fear, my son," said Cornstalk composedly, "the Great Spirit has sent you here that we may die together."

He rose calmly as the murderers burst into the room, and the next instant fell with seven bullets in his breast. Ellinipsico "continued still and passive, not even raising himself from his seat," and so met his death.

But this is in advance of our story.

One chief of them all did not come to take part in the treaty making on the Scioto. That was the other great chief, Logan. When messengers were sent to summon him, he returned answer that he was a warrior, not a councillor. But as he would not come, Lord Dunmore sent to him an emissary, one named John Gibson, a man who had lived among the Indians, knew their language thoroughly, and who was to a great extent in their confidence. Gibson at the time took down literally what Logan said to him, and afterwards stated that he had added nothing. The warrior said:

"I appeal to any white man to say if he ever entered Logan's cabin hungry and he gave him not meat; if he ever came cold and naked and he clothed him not? During the course of the last long and bloody war, Logan remained idle in his camp, an advocate of peace. Such was my love for the whites that my countrymen pointed as I passed and said, 'Logan is the friend of the white man!' I had even thought to have lived with you, but for the injuries of one man. Colonel Cresap [A mistake. Colonel Cresap had nothing to do with it], the last spring, in cold blood and unprovoked, murdered all the relations of Logan, not even sparing my women and children. There runs not a drop of my blood in the veins of any living creature. This called on me for revenge. I have sought it. I have killed many. I have fully glutted my vengeance. For my country I rejoice at the beams of peace; but do not harbour the thought that mine is the joy of fear. Logan never felt fear. He will not turn on his heel to save his life. Who·is there to mourn for Logan? Not one!"

Those who were present when John Gibson read this speech to the rough bordermen say that they were so greatly impressed by it that for days they talked it over around their campfires; and continually tried to say it over to each other.

The frontiersmen were disappointed. They had hoped to be able to carry the war further into the enemies' country; and they came close to mutiny when ordered to countermarch. But the job was done. It was just before the Revolutionary War, and there is no question but that it kept the tribes quiet through the first two years of that struggle, and so permitted the white man to get a foothold beyond the mountains. If it had not been for this, in all probability our boundaries would have been fixed, when peace was negotiated, at the Alleghany Mountains; and Great Britain would now own all our West as she owns Canada.

A writer named Hutchins gives an interesting glimpse of the delivery of captives by the Indians:

"The Indians delivered us their captives with the utmost reluctance, shed torrents of tears over them, recommending them to the care of the commanding officer. They visited them from day to day, brought them meat, corn, skins, horses, and other matters, that were bestowed on them while in their families, accompanied with other presents and all the marks of the most sincere and tender affection. Nor did they stop here; but when the army marched, some of the Indians solicited and obtained permission to accompany their captives to Fort Pitt, and employed themselves in hunting and bringing provisions for them on the way."

CHAPTER XI

THE claims of the Algonquin branch to the lands south of the Ohio River being thus extinguished, there remained only the very shadowy claims of the Cherokees on the other side. If the Cherokees could be satisfied, then there would be at least a formal peace throughout the Kentucky country; and Daniel Boone could revert to his pet scheme of leading settlers into the new land without fear of a concerted effort to wipe him out, and with only the usual and inevitable small parties of marauders to cope with. There is no doubt that he would on his own account have organized another expedition similar to the ill-fated first attempt, but this proved unnecessary. At this moment a soldier of fortune with a grandiose vision of his own came to the front.

This was a man named Henderson. He had started life as a constable, but had soon worked up to be a judge of North Carolina. Contemporaries describe him as of great eloquence, both in public speaking and in conversation; of an agreeable and expansive personality; rather too lavish with his money. In short, he was a typical promoter; and in these days would be booming real estate near Los Angeles, or wild-catting new districts for oil, or taking up far water rights in inaccessible mountains—and all on a big scale. In those days he conceived the idea of "buying" Kentucky from the Cherokees, offering the land to settlers on good terms, and so becoming the proprietor of a true kingdom. There were any amount of holes in the scheme. In the first place, the Cherokees could be said to own Kentucky only by a wide stretch of the imagination. In the second place, Virginia had every legal right to consider it a part of her back country. In the third place, it was illegal because a general law required the formal assent of governors and assemblies of the different provinces to ratify the purchase of any lands whatever from Indians.

These things worried Henderson very little, though as a judge he must have been perfectly aware of them. He had several pretty good antidotes to all these facts. As, for instance, this was in the year 1774, just before the Revolution, and the royal governors were probably too busy near home to bother about an expedition into the remote wilderness: the settlers knew nothing about the legal aspects of the matter, but any one could safely bet they would not peacefully give up their land on any account once they had made their homes on it. At any rate, Judge Henderson's glowing optimism found seven others like himself with some capital, and the eight of them set eagerly about the business.

The first thing to do was to deal with the Cherokees; and the man selected for that job was Daniel Boone. Some maintain that Boone and Henderson had worked together on this scheme from the start; and that all of Boone's solitary adventuring had really been on behalf of this very scheme; but it seems much more likely that the reports the Hunter brought back suggested the idea to Henderson's quick imagination. It was natural that the men should get together, for their desires were now the same.

Boone and Henderson at once visited the Cherokee towns, making their proposals. The Indians delegated one of their chiefs to return with the white men to examine the goods they offered as a purchase price. These consisted of about fifty thousand dollars' worth of arms, clothing, trinkets, and rum, which Henderson had collected in one spot, and which no doubt made an imposing show when heaped up in one or two cabins. At any rate, the delegate reported favourably, so Oconostota, the greatest of the Cherokee chiefs, issued a call to his tribesmen to assemble for the treaty. They gathered at a place called Sycamore Shoals, some twelve hundred strong; and after considerable dickering and speech making the Treaty of Sycamore Shoals was signed by which was made over all the land between the Kentucky and the Cumberland rivers. There was considerable reluctance on the part of the Indians: and the signing was accompanied by warnings that the chiefs would not pretend to be guarantee against irresponsible acts by the younger warriors.

"Brother," said old Oconostota to Boone, "the land beyond the mountains is a dark ground, a bloody ground."

"Brother," said another chief, called Dragging Canoe, "there is a black cloud hanging over that land. We have given you a fine land, but I believe you will have much trouble in settling it."

Indeed there was dissatisfaction almost immediately; for though the goods looked imposing in one pile, when divided each individual's share was very small. One warrior came forward exhibiting as his share of the whole transaction one shirt!

"In a single day on this land we have sold," he complained, "I could kill enough deer to buy me a shirt like this!"

Nevertheless, the treaty seems to have been fairly come at. The Cherokees knew perfectly that they had no real title to the country; they knew that this "sale" would not prevent their hunting there as long as the game lasted. It is recorded that, unlike most of this bargaining, no liquor was permitted until the discussions were over.

Nor did Henderson care much about the validity of the title. All he wanted was some sort of a paper to go on. Immediately he sent Boone to cut a route through to the new possessions.

The Scout picked thirty of the best backwoodsmen to be had, and with them at once attacked the construction of the famous Wilderness Road which for many years thereafter was to swarm with the emigration to the West. It was at first, as these men made it, merely a trail, fit only for pack-horses; but its grades, the selection of its route through the passes and over the rough country is a testimony to Boone's practical eye and engineering knowledge. With great skill he took advantage of buffalo roads, Indian traces, his own hunter's trail, and the Warrior Path of the Indians, connecting them up, cutting through the forests and dense cane-brakes, blazing mile trees for distance. The job took them about ten weeks, which was very fast work, to reach the banks of the Kentucky River, where they thought their main troubles were over. But the Indians had been watching this invasion with growing uneasiness. The defeat at the Kanawha and the Treaty of Sycamore Shoals prevented them from any formal declaration of open war; but small bands were afoot, and before daybreak one of these attacked Boone's party. They managed to kill a negro servant and wounded two men, but were then driven off by the axemen.

There was no further trouble for the moment. Boone's party pushed on to the place he had long since picked out as a site; and there started to put up cabins, and commenced a stockade. As they drew near the ground Boone had selected a great herd of buffalo made off, a wonderful sight, with the grown beasts compactly in the centre and the young calves playing and gambolling about on the flanks. Soon after Boone's party came other small bands of adventurers spying out the land, selecting homesites, and also beginning to put up stockades. The immigration had begun, although the first-comers were all merely forerunners, without their families or household goods. They were all equally delighted with the country, amazed at the swarms of game.

But now the hovering bands of Indians began to strike. The white men were so eager to go hunting; to find themselves plots of land; to do this, that, and the other, as you or I would be in like circumstances, that they were apt to skimp such hard drudgery as cutting logs and putting up stockades. More white men could be expected soon, and if these first-comers wanted the pick of the land they must get very busy! And what live man could resist the lure of the buffalo, the deer, the elk, the turkeys and clouds of wild pigeons! As a result the defensive works were neglected. Even at Boonesborough, as the new post was named, Boone could not induce his men to complete the simple stockade. So when the small Indian war parties finally swooped they got results, and several men were, as Boone spelled it, "killed and sculped."

This brought about a panic among a great many of the newcomers. They had come into the country on the understanding that the Indians had made peace, and being "sculped" did not look very peaceful to them! A great many became panic-stricken and started back for Kentucky, for they had less than no relish to be caught in an Indian war. They had seen such things at first hand.

Boone himself was undaunted. He sent a letter to Henderson stating in unexcited terms the "sculping," that the "people were very uneasy," and advising him that it would be a very good idea if he would hurry up in support.

Boone had no information as to whether Judge Henderson had yet started on his way; but as a matter of fact, that vigorous and energetic gentleman, three days after the signing of the treaty, had left Wantaga with a party that included forty mounted riflemen, a body of negro slaves, forty packhorses, a drove of cattle, and a train of wagons with provisions, ammunition, seeds, farming implements—in short, all the necessities for a permanent settlement. He had even brought the materials for making gunpowder. The eight adventurers who were backing the scheme certainly had confidence enough to sink considerable money in it! Indeed, five of them in all accompanied the expedition.

At Powell's Valley, just below Cumberland Gap, they had to abandon the wagons, as was to have been expected, and to go forward with only the pack animals. In anticipation of this, probably, a post had already been established at Powell's Valley under Joseph Martin, in whose charge, for the time being, were left the heavy materials and the wagons.

Boone's messenger with his letter met them when they were fairly in Cumberland Gap. The party had been enjoying the usual difficulties of travel with numbers of packhorses in new and difficult country. It rained a great deal, and at times they encountered heavy snowstorms so thick that one of the men got lost. The trail was very steep. Much chopping away of down timber had to be done. The packs were always shifting or slipping, with the accompanying row and trouble and confusion.   There were many streams, most of them in flood.   One day they had to cross fifty times "by very bad foards," into deep water, with steep rotten banks down which the horses must be forced to plunge, and bad bottom that mired and threw them and all but drowned them.   Sometimes the packs had to be ferried across on rafts and the horses swum.   A packed animal in thick timber is always getting stuck between trees, turning his saddle and twisting his load.   In these forests it was a rare thing to find good grazing handy, and yet the beasts must be kept fed and strong.   Such an outfit, by its very nature, is vulnerable to attack, especially in a wooded mountain country that forces it to one definite route.   Scouts had to range far afield.   Were it not for the confidence that at last a real peace had been arranged with both the northern and southern tribes, you can readily see that such a journey would be filled with a deadly anxiety.

Nor were their day's troubles over with the making of camp.   In spite of the peace it was realized that precautions must be taken against small bands of marauders, so a nightly watch must be kept; no light matter for wearied men.   And then in the morning the packing must be done.

As everyone knows who has had anything to do with this sort of wilderness travel, one of the most annoying of the petty troubles is the straying of horses.   The animals must eat, after their heavy day's labour; and they must be turned loose to feed on the natural pasturage.   For a time, until the first of their hunger is appeased, they stay in a compact band near home; but after a while they begin to wander in search of choice bits. By morning they may be scattered over quite an extent of territory. This is not so bad for one who understands the habits of the beasts and can follow a spoor; but every once in a while a single horse will be seized with a travelling fit and will start straight out for somewhere indefinite. He doesn't know himself where he is going; but he is on his way. Sometimes he takes a little band of the others with him. He never travels faster than a slow, steady walk; but that gait can cover an aggravating distance if continuous.. When overtaken he stands still and looks at you with a mild surprise.

There is no way by which the delays caused by a search for strayed stock can be avoided when the journey is long. If you picket them anywhere but on a flat open plain they will soon tangle themselves up, or shorten their ropes so they have only a small circle in which to find grass. Hobbling may help in catching the horse; but a wise animal soon learns to travel nearly as well with hobbles as when free. If the animals are to be kept strong and fit for a long journey, they cannot be corralled at night, for grass is not as sustaining as grain and they must have every opportunity to fill up. So the wilderness traveller learns to read tracks, and makes up his mind that every once in a while he will be delayed in his day's journey.

A man named William Colk, who kept a most amusing diary of this trip, gives a vivid picture of some of this horse misfortune that might have been written of any trip to-day into the Rockies or Sierras:

"I turned my horse to drive before me and he got scard ran away threw Down the Saddel Bags and broke three of our powder goards and Abram's beast Burst open a walet of corn and lost a good Deal and made a turrabel flustration amongst the Reast of the Horses Drake's mair run against a sapling and noct it down we cacht them all again and went on."

And at this time of the year the plot was complicated by the abundance of yellow-jackets' nests.   When a horse stumbled against one of these and turned loose its vicious swarms there was always a grand stampede of man and beast.

Boone's message was a facer.   It shows how seriously these people took even the bare chance of an Indian war when I tell you that that very night several men started on the back track.   The next day the expedition encountered the first of numerous bands of refugees fleeing to the comparative safety of the settlements.   They were frightened to death, saw Indians behind every tree and devils in every shadow, and you can imagine each had a story wilder than the last.   They talked massacre, raid, and burning, and predicted that in a fortnight there would not remain a white man in Kentucky.   Henderson had the greatest difficulty in holding his own party together in the face of these alarms; and realized that it would be vitally necessary to get word to Boone at once that the slow-moving pack trains were on the way. A young man named Cocke gallantly volunteered to carry the message, and actually did so in the face of real and imagined dangers.

But our sturdy Hunter had no notion of being frightened out of the country, and his influence and reputation held with him most of the original party. There is no doubt but that, had it not been for him, Kentucky would have been deserted by the white man; and so, together with all our West, have been adjudged British in the settlement after the Revolution.

Henderson and his party reached the new settlement on the Judge's birthday, and were welcomed by the firing of rifles and loud shouts. There were now eighty people in the settlement; the Indian panic had been shown by the scouts to be based on the chance raids of a few small parties; Cornstalk, chivalrous as always, came out in strong denunciation of these outrages and vehemently ordered all warriors to keep away from the white man's country. The work of the new settlement was systematized. Hunters were deputed from the sixty-five riflemen to supply game. This was no light matter, for already, owing to skin hunting and the movement away from the fort of the game herds, the hunters had to range fifteen or twenty miles away in order to encounter wild animals in the desired numbers. Of course there was what we would call abundance nearer home; but these men wanted meat quickly and in quantity. Other members of the community planted corn, working in common, appearing every morning at a blast of a horn and alternately labouring in the fields or standing guard as the "captain" directed.   Still others, under Boone himself, chopped out a clearing: felling trees, shaping and notching logs, splitting clapboards and "shakes," hewing puncheons, in preparation for the building of a real fort and stockade, and comfortable cabins for those who were to follow.

This fort was typical of the times.   It stood on a slight elevation, not far from the river banks, and consisted of an enclosure two hundred and fifty feet long by a hundred and seventy-five feet wide.   The cabins, of which there were about thirty, were built so that the backs of them formed part of the walls of this enclosure.   They were of course pierced with loopholes, and their roofs pitched only one way, away from the back walls, so that a man could lie on the slope and shoot over the edge, and also so that firebrands hurled on top could be put out without exposure.   The spaces between the cabins were filled with the stockade walls.   To make the stockade, a deep trench must be dug; logs placed upright in the trench; the trench filled in and tamped down; and the cracks in the logs filled up to be bullet proof.   At each corner were two-story block houses with the upper stories projecting.   Wide gates were located opposite one another.

Now all this was, as you can readily imagine, a tremendous labour.   In view of the fact that Indian trouble, at least on any great scale, seemed to be settled and in view of the fact that other constructive necessary work was crying to be done, it is not surprising that in spite of Boone's best efforts the work dragged.

In May, the "fields" being planted, these backwoodsmen met under a great tree and formally organized themselves, adopting a constitution, passing laws, holding elections, all in due order. It is noteworthy that Daniel Boone had much to do with laws as to game protection and improving the breed of horses. Within a week the little settlement was thrown into great excitement by receiving news of the Battle of Lexington. The backwoodsmen were all patriots and enthusiastically pledged their support to the new cause; but at present there did not seem to be much they could do about it. In fact, just at this time, they were having all they could do to maintain themselves. The newly planted crops were still in the future; the provisions that had been brought were rapidly giving out; there was almost no salt; game was withdrawing from the immediate vicinity. There was no bread, so they pretended that the white meat of turkeys was bread. "Even big meat was none too easy to get," Mr. Ranck tells us, "but Judge Henderson's black Dan managed to keep a supply, and with some vegetables from the fort garden, 'cats' (catfish) from the river, and milk," they managed to get along.

The news of Lexington was valuable in one way: for both Boone and Henderson used a report that Lord Dunmore was trying to stir up the Indians to take sides with the British, to get the fort completed. All the cabins in the fort proper, however, were not continuously occupied.

The Wilderness Road

Some of the settlers preferred to live on their farms near by; but they all came in promptly enough at any alarm.

About a month later Boone, satisfied that at last the place was strongly enough fortified to justify trusting his family to it, set out to get them. His old friend Richard Callaway went with him, to do likewise; and also a party of men who were to bring back salt from the supplies in Powell Valley, where Henderson had left his wagons. Salt was by now very badly needed, not only for eating, but because of the impossibility of preserving wild meat in the warm weather without it. The men found the salt all right, but so distrustful were they of the wilderness, and so confident were they of Boone, that they squatted down in the Powell Valley to await his return with his family, and nothing would induce them to budge. Judge Henderson wrote in a letter: "Our salt is exhausted, and the men who went with Colonel Boone for that article have not returned, and until he comes the devil could not drive the others this way." Indeed this confidence was shared by many others, for when Boone started back with his people, his horses, his cattle, and his dogs, his provisions and household goods, he found himself joined by quite a number of other families bound not only for Boonesborough but for Harrod's new station, and two other small forts. Even after these had left him at "the hazel patch" in Kentucky he was still at the head of twenty-seven rifles. The older boys drove the cattle, which were usually in the lead to set the pace; the little children were packed in baskets made of hickory withes slung on gentle horses, or else packed between rolls of bedding. The scouts ranged the forest far and wide.

His return with these additions to the population—and the salt—was received with great rejoicings by the men left at Boonesborough. The infant settlement had lost heavily even of its first population. A good proportion of those who had first come out were merely adventurers for excitement, good hunting, and to satisfy their curiosity. When they had satisfied all these desires, they drifted back home or farther afield. Others had come out merely to file on claims of land, after which they returned to look after their genuine farms back home, intending to move to Kentucky later for permanent settlement. And of course there were the timid who were scared by the Indian rumours. At one time Boonesborough was actually down to twelve rifles! though the numbers fluctuated widely.

Boone's party arrived in early September. His wife and daughter, Jemima, were the first women to set foot on the banks of the Kentucky River. It is amusing to read of the immediate effect of the presence of the gentler sex on the bordermen. "The men, and especially the younger ones, immediately improved in appearance, for there was a sudden craze for shaving and haircutting," says Ranck. "An ash hopper, soap kettle, and clothes line were set up. Hickory brooms and home-made washboards multiplied. The sound of the spinning wheel was heard in the land, and an occasional sight could be had of a little looking glass, a

MAPLE SUGAR

patchwork quilt, knitting needles, or a turkey-tail fan."
And we can imagine the rapture of the youngest Boone
children at the sights to be seen and the things to be done.
Nevertheless, we can also imagine that Mrs. Boone and
Miss Jemima were glad, some weeks later, to see Richard
Callaway come in at the head of a party that included three
married women and quite a bevy of young ladies. The fort
began to look like a real settlement, with its houses, its women and children, its domestic animals and its planted
crops. Boone's dream had at last come true.

It is related that with Callaway came a man named Pogue
who was "an ingenious contriver." Nowadays he would
probably advertise as a Handy Man. These pioneers could
do the big things well, but were not so deft when it came
to making or mending spinning wheels, churns, washtubs,
piggins, and noggins. A piggin is a pail of which two of
the staves are longer than the others, and a cross piece is
fastened to them by way of a handle. A noggin is a
smaller vessel, also with staves like a pail, one of which
is left long, somewhat like a dipper with a perpendicular
handle.

The crops had come in. The women took up their regular occupations, the dairies, the cooking, spinning, weav-
ing, washing, carrying the water; the men assumed their
routine jobs of building, clearing, hunting, planting, culti-
vating, and the defense. In making the clearings the trees
must first be girdled, to deaden them; then felled, and cut
into logs that could be handled; then "rolled" out of the

way. The stumps were generally left; and they made wonderful individual breastworks, both for friend and foe, in wartimes. Everything seemed prosperous. Men continued to come in, some of them already famous, or destined to be so, such as Simon Kenton, the scout; George Rogers Clark, the hero-to-be of Vincennes; Benjamin Logan, the Indian fighter, and many others. The Indians were apparently resolved to fulfil the terms of the peace treaty. Two hundred and thirty acres of corn had been raised; the domestic animals were doing well; fruit orchards had been planted; laws made; there were twelve women in the country and close to two hundred men.

Then just two days before Christmas this peaceful content was rudely shattered. Two boys, named McQuinney and Saunders, crossed the river, and climbed the hills opposite the fort. They were just out for fun, and never dreamed of taking their rifles with them. The settlers had been so long undisturbed that only the old-timers went always armed. The boys had the bad luck to run across a little roving band of Shawnees. It is doubtful whether the savages considered themselves on the warpath; but the temptation of such easy prey was too much for them. Four days later, after much anxious search, the body of McQuinney was found in a cornfield about three miles away. Saunders was never heard of again.

The settlement was thrown into great grief and alarm. No man could tell what this portended. Scouting parties took the woods; the families moved in; men went armed;

the old, comfortable, easy life vanished. Only some time later was it known that the Indians numbered only a half dozen; that Cornstalk himself had gone to Fort Pitt to denounce them and disclaim responsibility; and that a general Indian war was not to be feared.

CANDLE DIPPING

CHAPTER XII

NEARLY seven months went by peacefully as far as Indians were concerned. Then on a still, hot, midsummer Sunday afternoon, following the customary Bible reading that replaced church, Jemima Boone and her friends, Elizabeth and Frances Callaway, took one of the elm- or birch-bark canoes and started out down the river. They had gone but a short distance when their craft struck a little sandbar running out from a point. This was no unusual occurrence, especially at such times of low water; and the three girls laughingly argued as to which should step off into the shallow water to shove the light craft adrift. At this instant five Indians darted from the thick canebrake at the water's edge and seized them.

So sudden and unexpected was this appearance that the

girls were dragged from the canoe and into the thick cover before they had gathered their scattered wits: and once there the threat of the tomahawk was enough to keep them silent. It is related that "Miss Betsy," the oldest, managed to smack one of the Indians on the head with her paddle before it was snatched from her hands.

The Indians rushed their captives at full speed up a thickly wooded ravine to the top of the high-forested hills that roughly parallel the river. There they took a more leisurely gait and struck out across country with the intention of hitting the "Warrior's Trace" that led to the Ohio River.

The girls' absence caused no uneasiness until milking time; which fact afforded the savages several hours' start. Then the alarm was sounded by one of the hunters who had paddled down river to meet them. The abandoned canoe and the plain trail to be read near the banks of the river clearly enough told the story. Immediately the fort was in a turmoil. Men were summoned; and shortly two parties set out—about twenty men in all—one, mounted, under the command of Callaway; the other, afoot, under Boone. Callaway with his horsemen pushed off to a crossing of the Licking River in hopes of intercepting the fugitives, if—as seemed probable—they should cross there. Boone and eight men, three of whom were lovers of the girls, were to follow the trail.

It was now so late that little could be done that night, except follow the plain tracks to the point where the Indians began to cover them. Even these expert woodsmen could not pursue in the dark forests after night had fallen. But next morning by daylight they were on the scent and for thirty miles they puzzled out a trail blinded by every savage ingenuity. It is a striking example of the woodcraft of these men; for they not only followed the trail, but they must have followed it at high speed to have travelled faster than the Indians in flight. They were considerably helped by the ingenuity of the girls, who tore off bits of their clothing and left them on bushes whenever they could do so without discovery by the Indians' sharp eyes; broke twigs; or dragged their feet. To do this without the knowledge of men as keen as Indian warriors was a triumph in itself. Boone now decided that the Indians would be travelling less cautiously, so he boldly struck across country in what he considered the probable direction of flight, thus gaining some miles, if his reasoning was correct. It proved to be so. The tracks were discovered in a buffalo path; and there was now no attempt at covering the trail.

Much encouraged they pushed on more rapidly. Ten miles farther on they caught sight of the Indians making camp.

This was a welcome sight; but the next procedure had to be carried out with the greatest caution. No one knew better than Boone that the Indians' first act, in event of a surprise, would be to attempt to murder the captives. The girls, "tattered, torn, and despairing" were huddled at the foot of a tree only a few feet from the fire. Boone selected three of the most skilled of his men; and the four crept inch by inch nearer the fire. They were advancing against the sharpest, the most highly trained senses in the world, and every man there knew that a single false move, a solitary broken twig, even the rustle of a leaf would the next instant be followed by the crash of tomahawks on the poor girls' defenseless skulls. They held their breath in an agony of suspense. The advance seemed to consume hours. Finally, at the signal, the four men fired, and the others rushed forward with yells. Two of the Indians were killed and the other three were so completely surprised that, as one of the participants writes: "We sent them off without their moccasins, and not one of them with so much as a knife or a tomahawk."

When the rescuers returned in triumph to Boonesborough, they found that another band of warriors had during their absence burned an outlying cabin belonging to Nathaniel Hart, and ruined his young apple trees. Hart was with the rescuing expedition. The scouts and hunters began to bring in news of other small parties of Indians outlying around all the other settlements. They were nowhere in any large numbers, but, on the other hand, the small forces were everywhere. It became evident that the old period of security was over. The outlying settlers moved into the stockade, only venturing forth, armed, to tend their crops and their animals. Everywhere in the forest the Indians prowled singly or in small parties, watching for white men to shoot as one would watch for deer. They avoided contest as much as they could, lurking behind stump, rock, or tree until a sure and unexpected shot could be had. All night a solitary savage would lie behind some ambush to take a shot at the first man to emerge from the fort in the morning, and then with a wild yell, whatever the result, would disappear into the forest. Everywhere the settler found his cattle and horses driven off and his sheep and hogs shot down with arrows, for although the Indians were by now well armed with rifles, they carried bows and arrows for this purpose in order to save precious ammunition.

Of course, the usual precipitate emigration of the more timid at once began. Three hundred were said to have returned across the mountains; and the entire military force of Kentucky was reduced to about a hundred. There were only twenty-two armed men left in Boonesborough.

Nevertheless, all was not dark and gloomy. Three weeks after the rescue just described Squire Boone, in his capacity of Baptist Elder, was called upon to officiate at the marriage of Samuel Henderson and Betsy Callaway. This was the first wedding in Kentucky. Incidentally, within the year Frances Callaway and Jemima Boone married John Holder and Flanders Callaway, two of the young men who had helped rescue them. At the wedding of "Miss Betsy" there was "dancing to fiddle music by the light of tallow dips, and a treat of home-grown watermelons of which the whole station was proud."

For some time thus the fires of warfare smouldered on

the frontier. British agents were everywhere inciting the Shawnees and Cherokees. The employment of savages and the adoption of a species of warfare that could not fail to be horrible was a blot on the British name and is the chief reason why the natural antagonism of the Revolution was deepened to a hatred that has lasted beyond its normal span.

In the meantime, the proprietory government of Judge Henderson came to an end. It was in direct conflict with the rights of the older colonies; illegal; and in the end irksome. Had Henderson been content to sell his land outright to the settlers he might have kept their support; but he made the mistake of charging them a certain rental each year in addition to the purchase price. This the independent borderers did not like, so when the colony of Virginia refused further to recognize Henderson's government there were no very strong objections raised. The Judge filled an important rôle in the history of our west.

That winter was a bad one, what with the ever-increasing Indian attacks, the bad news from the war, the constantly dwindling numbers of the whites, and the dread of what was probably to follow when spring, the usual time for the opening of the warpath, should arrive. Every few days brought accounts of fresh attacks, more deaths. Ten men met at Licking Creek by Indians and defeated; three killed. A large party attacked McClelland's fort, killing and wounding several men. Two men killed at the Shawanese spring. The Indians attempt to cut off a small party from the fort; four men wounded and cattle killed. A small party attacked and scalped Hugh Wilson. A large party attacked the stragglers around the fort. Such are a few of the entries in a diary of the time. In these difficult circumstances Boone's figure towers commandingly. He was described as having a "quick perception of expedients, much prudence and caution, unyielding perseverance, and determined valour, combined with superior strength and activity of person." Certainly he was looked to for advice, for encouragement, for help, and for leadership in every crisis. He had little assistance in the point of numbers, but great help in the quality of the men who remained. There were twenty-two riflemen at Boonesborough, sixty-five at Harrodsburgh, and fifteen at Logans; that was all. Boone organized a small scout corps whose business it was to keep in the forest, two by two, feeling cautiously in all directions for the enemy, reading the signs, and coming in to the settlements only for fresh supplies of ammunition or to report. Simon Kenton was the most skilful of these, and one of the most bold. He was a big powerful man, standing well over six feet tall in his moccasins, with blond hair and a frank, open countenance. Next to Boone he was perhaps the greatest scout of them all; and he fell short of Boone, not in skill or in courage, but in coolness and judgment. His life in the forest at this time was like a romance: sleeping out without fire, skulking through the woodland, hovering on the flanks of his enemies, striking when the moment seemed right, and thoroughly enjoying it all. Several times he was taken prisoner. Eleven times he ran the gauntlet. Again and again he was within an inch of torture and death, but always either escaped or was reprieved. Once the famous renegade Simon Girty recognized and took pity on him. And to him and his brother scouts and rangers in the forest was due much of the credit for the persistence of the whites. Again and again their timely warnings assembled the settlers in the stockades before the savages could accomplish their surprise.

The two men assigned by Boone as scouts for Boonesborough itself were Simon Kenton and Thomas Brooks. They had a big job, and they did it well; but two men could not always cover an entire countryside. Early in March a party of Shawnees under a celebrated chief named Blackfish were lurking just outside the clearing waiting for a chance. Kenton had known of their presence in the country, and was close on their trail, but could not arrive at the fort before them. He was too well acquainted with Indians to try to get in until after dark, when he succeeded in slipping safely past, but too late to prevent the killing of two of the garrison. On the twenty-fourth of April again the Indians surrounded the fort a hundred strong, and just at a time when Kenton was at home for some purpose. For some good reason that we do not know the white men thought this a small party. Men like Boone and Kenton were not easily deceived, and they knew the various Indian stratagems well. One of the simplest was to lure the garrison out of a fort in pursuit of a small party and then ambush it with a larger. Boone knew this as you know your alphabet. Therefore, there must have been some very good reason never recorded why he was deceived on this occasion. It looks as though the wily Blackfish must have outdone himself.

At any rate a man named Daniel Goodman was walking alone across the clearing outside the fort when an Indian, with a yell of triumph, leaped forward from behind a tree and tomahawked and scalped him. Unfortunately for the exulting savage Simon Kenton happened to be standing near the fort gate, and, as always with these scouts, he carried his rifle across his forearm. It was a long, quick shot; but Kenton dropped his man. At the report a half-dozen savages rose like quail and scattered for cover. Immediately the men of the garrison dashed in pursuit. It is probable, from the fact that Kenton was in the fort, that he had brought news of the customary small band, and that the large war party had followed in after their decoys. At any rate the white men were suddenly fired upon from all sides, and at once rushed upon by overwhelming numbers of savages. If the Indians had known enough to keep to rifle fire they would probably have killed every man, but the powerful white men, fighting in a compact group, were able to force their way back to the clearing. Kenton killed three Indians with his own hand.

At the first fire Boone fell with a shattered ankle. Instantly an Indian leaped from behind a tree, his tomahawk upraised. Two jumps took him to the prostrate man. In another instant the weapon would have crashed into Boone's skull, but Simon Kenton, ever ready, killed the Indian with one of his famous quick snap-shots. Then the scout lifted his helpless captain with one arm, and with the other fought his way back to the fort gate. It is recorded that when he laid Boone down, the great Hunter said—"Well, Simon, you are a fine fellow"; and it is further recorded that Kenton was as elated and proud of this as a dog with two tails. Which little incident is an illuminating commentary on both men. Having failed in their stratagem, the Indians withdrew.

The broken ankle laid Boone up for several months. Nevertheless, he was able to direct many a day-and-night defense from his room. You would think that a strict defensive would have suited the most exacting, but once these bold riflemen actually ventured clear to the Ohio River, had two little skirmishes and won both of them. This was just to show the enemy that they were still going strong; for with their small numbers they could not hope to accomplish much else.

Two weeks later the Indians made a really serious attempt. Kenton and Brookes this time managed to bring warning, so there was no surprise. But the savages came in great numbers, and evidently under good leadership, for they sent detachments to make demonstration against the other two stations in order to prevent their dispatching reenforcements.

Then commenced a most vigorous attack that continued without intermission for forty-eight hours. The Indians were as ten to one, and they kept up an incessant fire, and made unremitting attempts to burn down the stockade. The forest resounded with wild yells and the roll of musketry. Inside, the little force had not a moment's rest. The portholes must be continuously manned, the fire continuously maintained, so that no savage would be able to creep forward. The women fought side by side with the men, taking their turn at the portholes, melting bullets, loading the rifles and handing them forward, caring for the wounded, cooking the food. All the wiles and stratagems of siege warfare they had to guess and forestall. At the end of the forty-eight hours the Indians suddenly and quietly withdrew. After it had been thoroughly established by the scouts that this was not another stratagem the gates were thrown open and the famished cattle and the wearied defenders poured forth into the blessed open.

There were many similar attacks on the three remaining forts: all very much alike, but all exciting enough to the defenders, you may be sure. In the frontier annals are many striking tales of heroism. For example, one of these border stockades was once surrounded so suddenly and after so long a period of immunity that the settlers were caught with their water reservoirs nearly empty. As yet the Indians had not made their attack, nor even declared themselves, and were lurking in the forests round about awaiting the opportunity for a surprise. They did not yet know that the settlers were aware of their presence. Here was a terrible situation: without water the siege that was to follow was sure to prove fatal, not only because of thirst, but because without water it would be impossible to quench flames. At this juncture the women made a proposal.

"It is certain death for men to try to reach the spring," said they, "on the other hand, the Indians believe that they are yet undiscovered, so perhaps they would not attack us. It is usual for the women to get water, and if we go to the spring as we always do, they will then surely think we do not know of their presence. And as they hope to surprise the fort they probably will let us go and come."

It took a long argument to convince the men. They could not bear the idea of sending their wives, their daughters, their sweethearts out unprotected fairly into the hands of a cruel and merciless foe. Nevertheless, this was the only possible way, and at length it was agreed.

So all the women and girls, down even to the little things of five and six, took every utensil that would carry water and sauntered out from the fort to the spring. All must look natural. The least sign of fear or a suspicion that all was not as usual would bring on an instant attack. They must walk slowly, in little groups, talking and laughing carelessly. At the spring they must fill their utensils in due order, without haste, keeping up still their careless talk; and then at last they must return leisurely to the fort, not in the compact group that would give them comfort, but straggling naturally along. All the time they felt the glaring bright stare of the savages concealed behind the leaves of the thick undergrowth, sometimes so close that the mere outstretching of an arm would have sufficed to bring down the fatal tomahawk. Behind the logs of the palisades the white men, too, watched in an agony, holding their breath with suspense, ready at the first whoop to rush forth to sell their lives as dearly as possible. The very forest seemed to have fallen silent with the deadly portent. Yet these women and children played out their parts to perfection, so naturally and easily as to deceive an audience the most critical and hostile in the world. Only when they had reached the very shadow of the stockade did some of the littlest girls begin to crowd forward against their mothers' skirts.

Another incident at another place was not quite so happy. The stockade, after suffering considerable privation, was overjoyed to see approaching a relief expedition of men and packhorses, bringing with them munitions and provisions. So delighted were the settlers that they fired off all their guns at once by way of salute. This scared the horses so badly that they broke loose and ran away, provisions and all, and were never recovered!

On the 25th of July, however, the bad times were for the moment ended by the arrival of a hundred and forty-five men sent by Virginia and North Carolina in answer to Boone's urgent messages. The Colonies were having their hands full enough with the British at this time, and could ill spare even this small body of troops, but it was felt that the borderers had earned a little respite!

CHAPTER XIII

THAT respite they utilized in characteristic fashion. After assuring themselves a supply of meat by the hunting they had of late to accomplish by stealth, the hardy frontiersmen set out in numerous small expeditions to hunt Indians. These were literally hunting expeditions, and the men conducting them lurked in the forest as wolves lurk for prey. Many were the single combats; the stratagems; the surprises; the bold forays. It was about this time that Simon Kenton with two men, scouting in the heart of the Indians' own country north of the Ohio River, actually managed at night to steal all the horses from an Indian village, about a hundred and fifty in number. In spite of the encumbrance of driving such a band through wooded country they reached the banks of the Ohio safely on the morning of the second day. The river at that point was very wide and deep, and unfortunately a gale was blowing that raised quite a heavy sea. Kenton and his companions could not induce the animals to face the swim. They could of course have escaped easily enough, but with characteristic reckless obstinacy they kept on trying at different points. In this instance they cut it too fine: the Indians overtook them, one white was killed, one escaped, and Kenton was captured. It is interesting to know that our old acquaintance Blackfish was the chief of the Indians: and that the first thing he did was to make careful inquiry as to whether Kenton was acting under Boone's command to steal the horses, or on his own initiative. In one case it was an act of war; in the other just a plain stealing expedition. Kenton replied that he had done it of his own accord, and thereby entered into a long experience of torture and captivity.

Peck gives an interesting impression of Boone at this period:

"As dangers thickened, and appearances grew more alarming, as scouts came in with rumours of Indians seen here and there, and as the hardy and bold woodsmen sat around their campfires with loaded rifle at hand rehearsing for the twentieth time the tale of noble daring or hairbreadth escape, Boone would sit silent, apparently not heeding the conversation, employed in repairing the rents in his hunting shirt and leggings, moulding bullets, or cleaning his rifle. Yet the eyes of the garrison were on him. Concerning Indian signs he was an oracle. Sometimes with one or two trusty companions, but more frequently alone, as night closed in he would steal away noiselessly into the woods, to reconnoitre the surrounding wilderness; and in the daytime stealthily would he creep along, his trusty rifle resting on his arm, ready for the least sign of danger; his keen, piercing eyes glancing into every thicket or cane-brake, or watching intently for signs of the wily enemy. Accustomed to range the country as a hunter and a scout, he would frequently meet the approaching travellers on the road and pilot them into the settlement while his rifle supplied them with provisions. He was ever more ready to aid the community or engage in public service than to attend to his private interests."

These individual raids and combats had the effect of impressing the Shawnees. From the hilltops they had seen Colonel Bowman's reënforcements marching in. The Colonel, suspecting that such an audience would be watching, had skilfully deployed his men in such a manner as to make the most of their numbers. The Shawnees had returned with exaggerated tales. It must be remembered that as yet the peace treaty was supposed to be in force; however, it might actually be broken. The chieftains were not yet ready to come out openly on the British side, although they were accepting arms, ammunition, and presents.

But a new difficulty arose. Again the supply of salt at Boonesborough became exhausted. Owing to the constant alarms of the summer just past the variety of food had decreased until now venison, cornbread, and turnips were all that remained. This was a monotonous enough diet, but it was particularly insipid without salt. Sickness threatened. By Christmas the situation became desperate. The long journey over the mountains for such a commodity was appalling; and as it was now mid-winter, and as Indians were rarely on the warpath at that time of year, it was agreed that a party of the settlers should try boiling out a supply from the salt springs at Blue Licks. This was no light job. It was necessary to boil down from five to eight hundred gallons of the water to produce a single bushel. So you can imagine the time it would take to get an adequate supply with only makeshift cooking kettles.

Boone gathered a party of thirty men from the three forts, partly of the borderers, partly of the militia reënforcements. With a few packhorses carrying only the kettles, axes, and bedding they started out. For food they were to depend entirely on Boone's rifle. The winter was a severe one, and even at the salt making around the fire the little party suffered acutely. It hindered the work, but after some weeks they sent back three men with the laden packhorses. They got through safely, to the great joy of the people.

But about the second week in February the work came to an end with dramatic suddenness. The weather was intensely cold; so cold that when Boone, hunting in a blinding snowstorm, encountered a large party of Indians, he was too benumbed to outrun the first dash of their young men.   With his characteristic good sense he offered no resistance whatever when once he saw that resistance would be useless; but dropping the butt of his long rifle on the ground he laughed good-naturedly as though the joke were on him.   Instantly he was surrounded by a large war party, curious, triumphant, overjoyed, for Boone was instantly recognized.   Indeed, in this party were his captors of eight years before, who laughed heartily at finding him again in their hands.   The Indians shook his hand, patted him on the shoulder, called him "brother," for so famous was he on the border that the savages would rather have captured him than George Washington himself.   In the meantime, Boone's keen brain, behind his careless exterior, had been swiftly noting details.   He saw that this was a war party by its paint and equipment, that it was a serious war party by its numbers, and that it was an important war party by its discipline, its leadership, the presence with it of two Frenchmen, and the fact that contrary to all custom it had taken the warpath in the dead of winter.   There could be no doubt that the expedition had a definite object; and that object could be no other than the capture of Boonesborough. Also there could be no doubt that the Indians must have been made aware that so many of the garrison were away. Indeed, the fact that they apparently had intended to pass by the salt-makers without attempting to gather their tempting scalps proved plainly enough the singlemindedness of their purpose and the danger of Boonesborough.

All these things Boone saw clearly as he leaned on his long rifle and smiled in the faces of his enemies: and in that few moments he made up his mind to a course of action. He knew not only the fort's weakness in numbers, but that one side of its stockade was even then in the course of reconstruction. The presence of the women and children at the fort made the merest chance of its capture unthinkable.

Boone greeted the chief of the Indians, our acquaintance Blackfish, with cordiality. His manner under the fierce scrutiny of the crowding warriors showed no trace of fear nor even of uneasiness; nor did he appear to the closest inspection as other than a visitor among them. By some means he managed to convey the idea, and to get it believed that he was on the whole rather glad to be captured, that he was wearied of fighting and would not be averse to a life of peace with his old enemies. As it was well known through all the tribes that Boone had always fought fairly and justly and without hatred, as his reputation for equitable dealing and wisdom was as well established as his renown as a fighter, in some way he managed to gain complete credence. He then went on to persuade them that it might not be impossible to arrange that all his people at Boonesborough would rather live farther north, among friendly Indians, than here on the dark and bloody ground, exposed to constant danger and alarm. He proposed that they test him by allowing him to persuade the salt-makers to surrender peaceably. Then he suggested that in the spring, when the weather was warmer, they should all return to Boonesborough properly equipped with horses to carry the women and children. Thus the whole settlement would be content to move north, to live thenceforth as the adopted children of the Shawnees. This he made sound entirely reasonable. His extraordinary influence over the Indians always has excited much wonder; but it was simply that he possessed all the qualities they particularly admired, and was in addition calm, just, and merciful.

After a long conference he succeeded in influencing Blackfish to turn aside for the purpose of gathering in the salt-makers. In return for a promise of good treatment for them all Boone guaranteed they would surrender peaceably. When within a short distance of the camp Boone was permitted by the Indians to advance alone—which in itself shows confidence in his word—to talk with his comrades. The latter agreed to follow his advice implicitly —another evidence of confidence, this time on the part of the white men—and so laid down their arms and surrendered.

There was difficulty now. Many of the Shawnee warriors claimed that in this negotiation they had not been consulted: they had come far on the war path, and they were loth to turn back now without scalps. A council was called, which lasted two hours. Blackfish struggled vehemently in debate. Boone was asked again to state his plan, which he did through the interpretation of a negro named Pompey, who was now a member of the tribe. At last it came to a vote. The question never involved the killing of Boone himself, but was as to whether or not the salt-makers should be killed. The war club was passed from one warrior to another. If he struck the ground with it he voted for death; if he passed it silently to his neighbour he voted for clemency. Fifty-nine struck the earth; sixty-one passed the war club!

But though the vote was so close, the decision was accepted as final; and thereafter the captives were scrupulously well treated.

They journeyed back at once to the Indian town of Old Chillicothe, and even Boone says it was an uncomfortable journey, for the weather was still very cold. They arrived on the eleventh day. As usual, when returning with captives, the war party stopped outside the town to dress and paint, and to strip a pole on the end of which was hung a "conjuring bag" containing locks of hair from each of the prisoners. Then Blackfish gave three yells, and the band began to sing and to dance around the stripped pole. At once the squaws and boys rushed out to the scene of celebration, while the warriors who had remained at home from the expedition retired in dignity to the council house. The squaws carried in the baggage, leaving the arriving warriors, in their gala paint, free to make a grand entrance, and to dance around the town's war post. This they did for about twenty minutes, after which they entered the council house with their prisoners.

This and more elaborate ceremonies took place always.

Blackfish was exceedingly proud of the numbers and quality of his prisoners.

After Chillicothe had admired to its heart's content he began to desire further praise. A grand tour was devised, ending at Detroit, then the British headquarters. They took Boone and ten other white men and started out as a sort of travelling circus with exhibits. Everywhere they received good treatment, and at the end of twenty days arrived in Detroit.

All this time Boone with his infinite patience and infinite sagacity never ceased for one moment to impress himself in the good graces of the savages. In this he succeeded better than he expected, rather too well, as it turned out. Boone was everything a savage admired. He was quiet and silent, and it must be confessed that the average borderer was apt to be noisy and brawling. He was brave; and yet he used the sense of prudence. He was especially endowed with that considered and deliberate wisdom so desired by the red man. But especially he was "always willing to deal with the Indians as having manhood and humanity about them, instead of waging a war of extirpation, as against wild beasts." In fact, so closely did Boone approximate the Indian ideals of virtue, and in so genuinely friendly a man-to-man fashion did he always deal with them, that it was said of him that "the Indians could not imagine how Boone could be a perpetual foe to them." Without doubt they believed at this moment—under his careful teaching them so to believe—that as he was so nearly an Indian in virtue he could not fail to wish to be an Indian in fact!

They stayed at Detroit for about a month, camping, as was usual with the Indians, outside the works. At this time Hamilton was commandant, and under him were many officers, and with them white women of rank. In its small way this was a brilliant society. To the Shawnee chieftain it was a prideful matter to have this celebrated prisoner to show off as his property. And the prisoner was indeed celebrated. The English crowded to view him as a curiosity; but seem to have capitulated to the simplicity and directness and charm of his character, for almost immediately we see the rough frontiersman being sought and entertained by the most exclusive of these English gentlemen and ladies, people usually profoundly contemptuous of "the uncouth and illiterate backwoodsmen." Indeed shortly we see them further giving a more substantial guarantee of their interest. Governor Hamilton himself tried to ransom Boone from his Indian captors, and gradually raised his price to one hundred pounds sterling, which was an enormous sum for such a purpose in those days and at the value money then bore. But Blackfish steadily refused. As we have hinted, Boone had only too well succeeded with his captors. He had not only gained their confidence but their affection. Blackfish flatly refused to ransom him at any price. As the British alliance with the Indians was hanging in the balance, Hamilton did not dare press the matter. The other white men were freely left as prisoners of war with the British, a fate infinitely preferable to what would have happened to them if Boone had not made terms for them. But Boone himself they intended to keep. This attempt at ransom having proved a failure, the English officers made up a sum of money which they offered the Scout as a gift for his immediate necessities. Boone declined this kindly offer with gratitude, but with dignity, saying simply that he "looked forward through the probabilities of his life, and saw no prospect of his being able to repay."

The savages, with Boone, returned over the hard and difficult journey to Old Chillicothe. Then they settled down, and Boone was adopted into the tribe.

CHAPTER XIV

THE ceremony of adoption was very formal, and somewhat painful. Blackfish himself proposed taking the Scout into his own family where, as Boone himself says, "I became a son, and had a great share in the affection of my new parents, brothers, sisters, and friends."

First of all, an old Indian squatted down in front of him and began slowly and ceremoniously to pull out all his hair, with the exception of the scalp lock on the crown; "as if he had been plucking a turkey," James Smith describes the process. "He had," Smith adds, "some ashes on a piece of bark, in which he frequently dipped his fingers in order to get a firmer hold." The scalp lock was then divided into three parts, two of which were wrapped about with narrow beaded bands, and the third was braided and ornamented with silver brooches. Next Boone was instructed to re-

move his clothes and put on a breech clout.   His face and
body were painted in ceremonial colours and patterns, and
he was ornamented with a neck belt of wampum, and silver
bracelets and armlets.   All this took place within the house.
The chief then took him by the hand and led him into the
street and uttered rapidly several times the alarm yell.   Immediately the whole village came running.   Still holding
Boone by the hand Blackfish made a long speech, after
which the new member was taken by the women of his Indian family to the river where he was scrubbed thoroughly
from head to foot.   This was supposed to wash out the
white blood.   He was given a white staff ornamented with
deers' tails and returned to the lodge of his captor, Blackfish.   In the case of the usual captive the family then had
a choice of whether he should be killed or adopted; but as
this had already been decided, Boone was taken to the great
council house.   This was a long structure without parti-
tions, with a door at each end over which was drawn the
totem animal of the tribe, and on the doorposts of which
were carved the faces of old men, emblems of gravity and
wisdom.   Running the length of the walls were raised
benches or bunks covered with mats of rushes.   Here other
members of the tribe had already brought presents of
clothes.   Besides the useful hunters' garments and blankets
were other things, such as—it is James Smith again who
tells us—"a new ruffled shirt, which I put on, also a pair
of leggings done off with ribbons and beads, likewise a pair
of moccasins and garters dressed with beads, porcupine

quills, and red hair—also a tinsel lace cappo." Now Boone's face and body were again painted, in new colours and designs, and a bunch of straight red feathers tied to his scalp lock. He was presented with a pipe, a tomahawk, flint and steel, and a tobacco pouch, and made to seat himself on a bearskin. Next entered into the council house all the warriors of the tribe, in ceremonial paint, and wearing all the finery they owned. These seated themselves in a circle along the walls of the council house, and for a time there was a profound silence while the smoke curled upward from the calumets. Then at length Blackfish arose and made a speech.

"My son," said he, "you are now flesh of our flesh and bone of our bone. By the ceremony which was performed this day every drop of white blood was washed out of your veins; you were taken into the Shawnee nation and initiated into a warlike tribe; you are adopted into a great family, and now received in the place of a great man." [Smith's report again. The new member was supposed to fill in the family the place of an Indian who had been killed.]

"You are now one of us by an old strong law and custom. My son, you have nothing to fear; we are now under the same obligations to love, support, and defend you that we are to love and defend one another. Therefore you are to consider yourself one of our people."

Personal introductions then took place, as at a reception. The evening was spent in feasting. Boone was given a bowl and a wooden spoon. The feast was of venison and corn boiled together in brass kettles, maple sugar, bear's fat, and hominy. Thenceforward no distinction was made between him and the other members of the tribe. "If they had plenty of clothing, I had plenty; if we were scarce, we all shared one fate."

Boone was named Sheltowee, or Big Turtle, and taken into the lodge of Blackfish. The chances of escape were practically nothing; so Boone, with his usual sagacity, so heartily entered into the life of the tribe and its occupations that he soon gained their entire confidence. In his own words: "I was exceedingly friendly and familiar with them, always appearing as cheerful and satisfied as possible, and they put great confidence in me. The Shawnee king took great notice of me, and treated me with profound respect and entire friendship, often entrusting me to hunt at my liberty." In this the Indians took only one precaution: they counted the bullets issued to Boone, and required of him a very exact accounting when he returned. Boone discovered that a half bullet with a light powder charge was accurate enough, if implanted in just the right spot, to bring down game at close range; so he cut his bullets in two, took especial pains in his stalking, and thus managed to accumulate a store of ammunition under the Shawnees' very noses.

He went often on beaver-hunting expeditions, for the severe winter was very favourable for capturing these animals by other than the usual trapping methods. The beavers, as you know, live in conical-shaped "houses," the entrances to which are under water. They have passages in the river banks called washes. The procedure was to break in the roofs of the houses, whereupon the beavers betook themselves to the washes whence they were pulled out by hand. It took considerable address to seize them without being bitten! The hunters also looked for holes where the bears were hibernating. They preferred to find the male bears, and could distinguish because the holes occupied by the males were always next the ground, while the females picked out their winter quarters high up for the safety of the cubs which were born near springtime.

In the village itself he took part in the various dances—the calumet dance, the chief's dance, the dead dance, the marriage dance, the sacrifice dance. He observed the marriage customs: where the suitor brings his gifts to the bride's parents, leaving them for consideration. If the bride's relatives, all assembled in council, confirm the match, they return the visit, bringing presents and also the girl herself; but if they disapprove, or the young lady is not willing, they return the suitor's own gifts by another messenger. He also entered into the various games; and here he proved his diplomacy and his knowledge of Indian character. "I was careful not to exceed many of them in shooting; for no people are more envious than they in this sport. I could observe in their countenances and gestures the greatest expressions of joy when they exceeded me; and, when the reverse happened, of envy." He also allowed himself to be distanced in the races and beaten in the ball games; not always, but more often than not, so that the vanity of the savages was gratified. In hunting, however, he allowed full scope of his skill and genius; which were so remarkable, even among these experts, that shortly he was being used as a sort of official meat provider. He made several quite long expeditions; and, as always, kept his eyes open and made observations that might prove useful to future settlers. "I find," he says, "the land, for a great extent about this river, to exceed the soil of Kentucky, if possible, and remarkably well watered."

Always Boone entered heartily and with genuine interest in the life as it was lived by the Indians. He took part in the games of lacrosse. Some of these, the less serious, were contested between the men and the women. In concession to their weaker sex the women had the privilege of picking up the ball and running with it; which was not permitted the men. On the other hand, the men were allowed to catch and shake the squaws to make them drop the ball! Boone also played atergain, which is a game played with beans, a number of which are placed in a bowl. One of these beans is marked, and is called the chief. The player shakes the bowl and tries to make the chief hop out, but with a loss of as few of the other beans as possible. When he has caused the chief to leap out, he gains as many points as there are beans left in the bowl. It takes considerable skill, and is a lot of fun. Try it. Another game was to shoot arrows at a rolling hoop. This was done both horseback and afoot; and the object was not to shoot through the centre of the hoop, but to split the rim. An expert at bow and arrow could hit a ha-penny at fifteen yards, we are told.

In the spring the Indians, recollecting the occupation of the whites when captured, took Boone to a salt spring on the Scioto and set him to boiling out salt. It was hard and monotonous work, not at all to the taste of an Indian warrior; but Boone, with his usual equable philosophy, worked patiently and efficiently at it. He was only lightly guarded, but he was guarded; and after due consideration of all the chances he decided against an attempt to escape, and returned to Chillicothe. He had now been in the Indian town over four months, in all of which time no faintest indication had been observed that he was not entirely satisfied with his lot.

To his alarm, during his fortnight's absence, preparations had been well forwarded for another expedition against Boonesborough. Nearly five hundred warriors had gathered; and the ceremonials that preceded a serious warpath were well under way. In the great council house the elders were gathered daily making their plans; delivering speeches. With each speech the orator presented belts of wampum, one belt for each point he wished to have remembered, generally of white and black; the white made from pieces of the inside of conch shells, the black from mussel shells. Outside the council house the younger men danced around the war post and struck their tomahawks into it, while the women, crooning, patted the drums in rhythm.

For three days they would fast, drinking only the war drink of bitter herbs and roots. During that time no warrior could sit down, or even lean against anything, until after sunset. The simple provisions for the journey were already prepared—corn and maple sugar. These would be in the control of men called *etissus,* who would parcel them out rigorously. No one would touch a mouthful of anything, either of the supplies carried nor of the provisions procured on the way, except by permission of the *etissus.* The waterproof gun covers of loons' skins were in place. The war budget was made up: a bag containing some one article from each man, the skin of a snake, the tail of a buffalo, a martin skin, a bird skin, or what not. On the march this budget would always be carried at the very head of the file by a designated official. When the party halted, the budget was laid on the ground, and no one was permitted to pass ahead of it without authority. This was as a measure of discipline. There were other prohibitions, too, all of them practical; such as that no one was allowed to lay his pack on a log, nor converse about women or home. And there were other rigid ceremonies on the warpath: as, for example, when a beast was killed for food its heart was cut small and burned on an especial fire, and nobody must step across this fire nor go around it except in the direction of the sun. Then when the time came for attack, the budget was opened and its contents distributed to their owners, who attached the articles to the part of the body established by tradition for each. After the battle the budget was reassembled, and the man who took the first scalp now had the privilege of carrying it. After the return he could suspend it before his door for one month; a great honour.

Promptly at the end of the three days of fasting Boone knew that the war party would set forth no matter what the weather. It was a bad omen otherwise. In single file, at spaced intervals, the painted warriors would move from the town, firing their rifles slowly one after the other, beginning at the front and progressing shot by shot to the rear. Once out of hearing of the town, however, a rigid silence was imposed. Now the expedition was launched for success or failure. Nothing could interfere with it unless someone dreamed an unpropitious dream; or unless a certain species of bird came and sang near an encampment. This bird the Indians called the Kind Messenger because it thus brought them warning that the expedition was not lucky. In either of the cases mentioned they always turned back unquestioningly.

Boone knew that his time was short and that if he were to act, it must be at once. No longer could he afford to wait for what he might consider a propitious moment. He took part in the councils and the war dance; as to the conduct of the campaign he even made one or two practical suggestions that were approved. Not by a word or look did he indicate that he was anything but pleased at the turn affairs had taken. The Indians were completely deceived.

On the morning of June fifteenth they doled out what they considered the day's supply of ammunition and sent him out to kill deer for the war party.   Boone pouched also the powder and half bullets he had been so long accumulating, and struck out boldly across country for home.

CHAPTER XV

THERE could hardly have been a more unpropitious time for an attempt at escape. Five hundred warriors, trained to the minute, were gathered; provisions were prepared. Instantly on the discovery of his flight Boone knew the whole pack would be on his trail. They knew the country thoroughly, with all its routes and also all its difficulties and obstructions. The course he must take would lead through forest, swamps, and across many rivers. If captured he could expect nothing but the torture, for the Indians could not fail to see in this attempt a deadly insult; and he now possessed many of their secrets and plans. His only advantage was his certainty of a few hours' start.

It was subsequently learned that his absence was discovered more quickly than he had hoped. The entire town was thrown into a commotion of rage. Immediately the

ESCAPE

fleetest runners and the keenest hunters were thrown out broadcast through the forest, while others began to puzzle out his trail; and still others loped off on what was considered his probable route. They guessed well. Boone found himself sorely pressed. He had to use his every art of woodcraft. He doubled and twisted and ran, travelling day and night, almost without rest, until the Ohio River should be reached. He dared not fire his gun, so his stored ammunition was of no use to him. He dared kindle no fire. He dared spend no time searching for even the poor food the barks and roots of the forest afforded him. Time and again his keen-eyed foes were literally all about him, but time and again he slipped through them. At length he pushed the bushes cautiously aside and looked out across the reaches of the Ohio River.

It was swollen by the rains, and its current swept by at mill-race speed. Even the strongest swimmer might well have despaired at this sight, and Boone was not a good swimmer. He had no time to cut a log and trust to the slow and uncertain process of kicking himself across, for the Indians were by now fairly on his heels. He descended to the shore, and there he found an old canoe that after going adrift at some unknown point far upstream had grounded here at his very feet to answer his great need! And out of all the hundreds of miles of the river course he had picked out this one point at which to emerge! Do you wonder that his simple faith was strong that he was "ordained by God to conquer the wilderness?"

The canoe had a hole in it, but Boone managed to make quick repairs of a sort good enough to get him across, though with some difficulty. Once on the other side he felt safe enough to shoot and cook a wild turkey, which is recorded as being the only food he tasted in his flight. One meal in five days: one hundred and sixty miles in five days.

He arrived at Boonesborough emaciated, gaunt, almost exhausted. His reception was enthusiastic, but he had to meet a great disappointment, for he had long since been given up as lost, and Rebecca Boone had gathered the remnants of her family and returned to Carolina. Boone speaks of his disappointment, and incidentally shows the great affection that existed between them. "Oppressed," said he, "with the distress of the country and bereaved of me, her only happiness, she had undertaken her long and perilous journey through the wilderness."

It would have been natural, after recuperating, for him to have followed her, and most men would have done so; but Boone, as usual, put his duty first. As he had feared, he found the fort in a bad state of repair. At once he set the inhabitants vigorously to work, and within ten days the stockades were renewed, new bastions had been built, the stores of provisions and water replenished, and all was prepared to resist a siege. The attack, however, delayed. Boone's escape had thrown the Indian councils into confusion. His arrival at the fort had of course been known and immediately reported back; as also his vigorous efforts toward putting the place in condition for defense. The chance for a surprise was gone; as also the advantage of moving against decaying works. A Grand Council of all the nation had been held. The elders restrained the impatience of the youths, pointing out that as the possibility of surprise had been lost, it would be well to make preparations so complete and accurate that success would be certain. More warriors were summoned; more ammunition collected. This expedition against Boonesborough was conceived and executed on a scale, and especially with a dogged persistence, that had never been equalled in Indian warfare. The siege that we shall soon see to follow lasted nine days; the longest single attack on record; and after its close the garrison picked up "a hundred and twenty-five pounds of flattened bullets that had been fired at the log stronghold —this salvage made no account of the balls thickly studding the walls."

However, that was later. Having finished putting the works into a state of defense, Boone, with his characteristic boldness, resolved to give the enemy something to think about. So he selected nineteen of the best woodsmen and with them set out on his back track into the heart of the enemies' country! His idea was not so much that he could inflict substantial damage as to impress the Indians, and to find out for himself what was really going on. Their only provisions were dried corn and maple sugar, like the Indians'. This daring foray actually crossed the Ohio River and penetrated to the Scioto River, where Boone had been employed in making salt. They managed for some time to avoid the savages, but at length ran across a party of thirty on its way to join the main army at Chillicothe. What Boone calls a "smart fight" ensued in the forest. Boone's nineteen proved too much for the thirty.

Now that his presence in the country had been discovered, he knew the place would soon be too hot for him. The twenty white men executed a masterly retreat, avoiding the scouts and light parties sent out to intercept them; and returned in triumph and safety to the fort. Simon Kenton and another man stayed behind to steal some horses, which was characteristic of that bold and restless spirit. In consequence he was not in the fort during the great battle, and that caused him profound grief!

CHAPTER XVI

ONE thing Boone's expedition had clearly shown: the calm interval did not mean that the Indians had abandoned their project. The warriors were gathered at the Shawnee town, and shortly they set forth under the command of Blackfish. There were four hundred and forty-four of them, and with them twelve whites as military advisers. The chief of these was a French Canadian, a lieutenant named De Quindre. A number of very important and famous chiefs were with the expedition: such as Black Bird, whom Patrick Henry called "the great Chippewa"; Moluntha, who had led the Shawnees in all the really serious invasions of Kentucky; and Catahecassa, who had led in Braddock's defeat. Pompey, the negro, was also along, valuable mainly because he spoke English, not otherwise highly considered, but a member of the tribe for all that. The equipment was that usual to an expedition of this kind, simple, confined to the rifle and the corn wallet for the warriors. But, contrary to the usual custom, almost incredibly contrary, was the presence of a number of pack-horses. They carried extra ammunition; but that was only in order that they might carry something. Their intended use was quite different. You remember that when Boone surrendered at the Salt Licks he gained immunity for his men by suggesting that in the warmer season it might be possible to move all the inhabitants peaceably to the Shawnee country there to live in adoption, and that he suggested, further, that packhorses be brought for the purpose of transporting the children and the household goods? Well, in spite of Boone's escape the savages seem to have retained some lingering hope that the original plan would be followed. They hated to give Boone up. They liked him, and they admired him. Even though appearances were now so strongly against him, they were loth to abandon entirely all thought of keeping him as one of their tribe.

This not only accounts for the otherwise unexplained packhorses, but also for the most extraordinary delays and negotiations that preceded the attack. Boone, as will be seen, made the most skilful use of these negotiations, prolonging the delays as much as possible. He had promptly, on his arrival, sent messengers to the settlements for reënforcements, and every moment gained was an added chance for the safety of the garrison.

Early in the morning of September 7th the Indian forces crossed the river and quietly took up their positions in the surrounding woods within rifle shot of the fort. Their advance had been reported by the scouts, so the garrison was prepared and within doors. To oppose the savage horde were thirty men: these, with the women and boys, were to make the place secure.

There was no attempt at concealment, and no hostile demonstration. The Indian elders had more than a strong hope that the place could be captured without a fight. They were very fond of Boone, and in spite of his desertion they knew that individually he was very fond of them, and that his enmity was only the enmity of loyalty to his own side. They had carried out honourably their agreements made when the salt-makers had surrendered to them the year before, and they believed that on that account the garrison would be inclined to trust any terms they might make now.

The forest lay as though empty, still and hazy in the autumn mists; the fort stood as though deserted, save for the rising of smoke from the rude chimneys of the cabins. Nevertheless, hundreds of fierce black eyes from the shelter of the leafy underbrush were scrutinizing every detail of the log fortress and the half-cleared ground that lay around it; and within the defenses eyes were at the portholes, and ears were strained to catch the least movement.

Suddenly the bushes parted and a solitary Indian, unarmed, and carrying a bit of white on a stick, advanced with composure to a point "within easy calling distance" of the fort, mounted a stump, and uttered the usual call of the woodsman, a prolonged hall-o-o-o! For a time there was no reply, and no signs of life in the fort. Boone knew too well the peculiarities of the Indian point of view to confess weakness by any undue eagerness, haste, or excitement.

After a sufficient pause had elapsed he sent back an answering hail.

The emissary could speak English. He announced merely that the chiefs desired a parley to consider messages brought from Governor Hamilton at Detroit. This was a most unusual opening for an Indian attack—customarily the first intimation was the war whoop and the rattle of rifles —but Boone was delighted. Negotiation meant delay; and delay meant a better chance for the arrival of the reenforcements from Holston. Consider for yourself the problem of defense that confronted him. The total length of the walls was nearly nine hundred feet, besides which there were the four corner blockhouses to be manned. Boone had at his command thirty riflemen, with an addition of about twenty boys. Spread out, that meant only one man to every thirty feet to be defended. The enemy outnumbered him more than ten to one, and was in force enough to deliver a formidable attack on all four sides at once, if they so desired; or to keep up a continuous battle by relays, night and day. Most men would have considered the job hopeless, and would have anticipated being overrun at the first assault. So you can readily understand that the leaders snatched at every chance for delay.

After a suitable and dignified silence Boone agreed finally to send three to meet three. All must be unarmed, and the meeting must take place beneath the guns of the fort. Immediately thereafter appeared Blackfish, the military leader; Moluntha, the "Shawanese King" so often mentioned by Boone during his captivity; and the Frenchman, De Quindre. To meet them went Boone, Callaway, and W. B. Smith. They carried with them only a calumet, or ceremonial tobacco pipe, and a piece of white cloth on a ramrod.

It is recorded that Boone found the meeting with Blackfish and Moluntha "embarrassing enough." Blackfish had made him a member of his family, and Moluntha had treated him with distinguished kindness: to which must be added that a real affection existed between them all. But the white man felt that he must be loyal to his own, and the Indians, in spite of their chagrin, respected him for it and admired the wiliness of his stratagem; for that was an Indian virtue. One source of heart-burning was speedily eliminated, however. Moluntha sorrowfully reproached Boone for killing his son "the other day over the Ohio"; but Boone energetically denied any knowledge of the act. The letter from Hamilton was then passed over and read. It contained terms for the surrender of the fort, and offered such favourable proposals that evidently the Indians thought they could not be refused, for when Boone had finished the perusal of the letter, old Blackfish patted him on the shoulder in a neighbourly fashion, saying:

"I have come to take the people away easily. I have brought along forty horses for the old folks, the women, and the children to ride."

"That is thoughtful of my father," replied Boone, apparently pleased. "But the road is long. It is a serious thing for all of a people to leave their homes. These things must be told them, and pipes must be smoked in council. Let not your young men or ours look upon the tomahawk nor the rifle. At the end of two days we will make reply."

To this proposal the three enemy emissaries gave assent, to Boone's great though secret satisfaction. Such delay had been beyond his most ardent hopes, and it was due solely to the esteem the Indians had conceived for the great Scout, and the hope that in some way he might be gained to their cause. After a peaceful and friendly stroll and conversation before the silent fort, the parties separated.

Inside the compound the entire garrison gathered about the returned emissaries. Boone briefly outlined Hamilton's proposals. He pointed out the odds against them, and the difficulties so few would encounter in trying to defend so large a place. He gave it as his opinion that the Indians meant to fulfil the terms they offered, and that the probabilities were strong that the garrison would arrive safely in the Indian country. Reënforcements had been sent for, but the time of their arrival was uncertain; if, indeed, they arrived at all. Those were the facts.

That was a different matter. The country was at war. The British were our enemies. Boonesborough was a fortress of the new republic. To accept Hamilton's proposals would not be to surrender as prisoners of war; it would be to desert to the enemy! For his part he felt it his duty to fight honourably for his own side to the death. There were elements of hope in the situation. The Holston men might come.   Did they hear Blackfish's statement of forty horses for the old folks and children?   That number meant that they thought Boonesborough more populous than was the fact.   The weakness of the defenders was unknown to them.   If they realized that but fifty rifles at most were available for defense, undoubtedly they would carry the place out of hand; but the Indian habit of warfare would not countenance a frontal attack against what they thought a large body of the deadly borderers.   If the weakness of the garrison could be concealed: and if all did a little better than they thought was their best, and if each kept up a stout heart, there might be a chance of winning through.

Whereupon, as a matter of course, they voted unanimously to reject Hamilton's terms; and at once turned to on the last details of preparations for defense.

Truth to tell, no one had the greatest confidence in the truce.   At any moment hostile demonstrations were expected.   Therefore everybody was surprised and delighted when small parties, sent experimentally to the springs, were not molested.   All the water was at once secured that could possibly be obtained without arousing suspicion.   The fort had its usual reservoirs, of course; but all the calculations of the time were for short attacks, lasting at most a day or two, and Boone rightly foresaw that this struggle, once joined, would be to a finish.   About sundown, again to the vast astonishment of the settlers, the cows and other live stock wandered out from the forest as they were accustomed to do every evening.   The savages had not molested them; and the settlers thankfully gathered them in. As soon as it was dark enough the most expert at concealment were sent out into the fort vegetable garden to bring in whatever was there either for man or beast. Within, everyone, even the women and small children, was busy cleaning and loading rifles, picking flints, moulding bullets, preparing defenses. There was intense excitement but no abatement of resolution. That night a sentinel stood on the lookout in every blockhouse; and every man slept at his station with rifle at hand. We have a record from one of them as to how literal was the well-known phrase, "to sleep on your arms."

"I had my powder horn and shot pouch at my side," he writes, "and placed the butt of my gun under my head. Five of our company lay on the east side of the fire, and T. and myself on the west. We lay on our left sides and my right hand hold of my gun."

But there was no alarm. The Indians honourably observed the truce. No more was heard or seen of them until the cool of evening on the second day, when again the bushes parted and the two chiefs and the Frenchman, bearing their white flag, came confidently forward to receive a reply that evidently they were certain would be favourable to their proposals.

"The garrison," said Boone, "has determined to defend the fort while a man is living." He then went on briefly to thank them for observing the truce.

The Indians, we are told, were deeply "astonished, disappointed, and exasperated" at this reply, so different from what they had confidently expected; but they listened with their customary gravity, and went back into the forest. Up to this point their proposals had been sincerely made. Now they turned to enmity; as indeed they had every reason to do honourably. And as what we now call treachery and stratagem were a legitimate and honest means of warfare, used without reproach by both sides alike, and indeed already employed by Boone, we can hardly join certain indignant writers in their horror at the next move. It was a game of wits, between wily and experienced players. Boone fought for delay, and used every means to get it; the Indians wanted possession of the stronghold and the people in it without a fight. From one point of view the safety of Boonesborough could be credited to an unknown Kentucky prisoner captured a short time before by the Shawnees. This man, when questioned, had informed his captors that the fort had "lately been reënforced with three companies each of seventy men." Against a possible two hundred and fifty riflemen the savages might well hesitate to deliver a frontal attack; whereas they would contemptuously sweep over thirty. And the conduct of Boone seemed to confirm this report of the Kentucky prisoner.

At the end of a short time, instead of the immediate assault the settlers now expected, came the three emissaries back with another proposal. This, unlike the first, was not sincerely intended, and was merely a means that was hoped to be effective in getting hold of the leading white men, and perhaps of the garrison itself. This time De Quindre did the talking through one of the other white men as interpreter.

He said that his orders from Governor Hamilton were to avoid bloodshed at all costs; he pointed out in corroboration of this the observance of the truce, the fact that the cattle had been allowed to enter the stockade; that what was really wanted was to remove the menace of Boonesborough against the British in the northwest; that therefore a surrender was not really necessary. What was wanted was peace on the border, so a treaty of peace signed by the leading men of Boonesborough would be sufficient; after which the savages would withdraw. He went on to suggest that the nine leading men of the garrison should meet with himself and the Indians to make such a treaty.

Boone, of course, had not much faith in this proposal. It might be the policy of the British, but here were half a thousand warriors come a long distance on a warpath, and it was against their nature to return empty handed. Still he possessed the confidence of Governor Hamilton; he had considerable influence and respect among the Indians; no one knew how far the military authority of the British in dictating the policy of such an expedition might extend. And above all here was a chance for further delay! The last consideration decided him. He agreed; but stipulated, "as it was now so late in the day," that the conference should not take place until the following morning; he also specified that it should be held in "the hollow at the Lick

Spring," which could be covered by rifle fire from the nearest bastion. The Indians withdrew.

At once Boone began to lay his plans. For the peace commissioners he selected men of long experience with Indians, and also of strength and agility. Among them were some of our acquaintance: Squire Boone, Richard Callaway, W. B. Smith, and Flanders Callaway who had married Jemima Boone. For the bastion he designated a number of the best rifle shots, whom he instructed to open fire promptly when any of the party waved a hat. Since to reach the Lick Spring the Indians must file by the fort, Boone ordered every human creature, women and children, white or black, to costume as a man and to make some sort of a showing at the pickets as though looking over in curiosity when the savages passed. "For that purpose," says Ranck, "every old hat and hunting shirt in the station was gathered up, and some new ones even were hastily manufactured. The next morning when Blackfish, De Quindre, the older chiefs, interpreters and attendants filed down to the meeting place they did not fail to note the large numbers of hatted heads that bobbed up at the top of the stockade to see them pass, and were disgusted at the apparent confirmation as to the strength of the garrison."

Boone and his men followed them unarmed, and the parties came together under the huge sycamores at the spring.

Fortunately for Boone's purpose of delay Indians are long on ceremonial and dignity, and love much talk, long flowery speeches, and due deliberation. The white men were invited to seat themselves on panther skins, and tobacco and whiskey were passed and discussed. Then a feast was brought on. It is related that "the besiegers sought with suspicious generosity to beguile the 'rebels' with eatables and drinkables from the British commissary department at Detroit, such as most of them had not seen, much less tasted, in many a long month." Then they proceeded to the business of making a peace, which was a very formal and complicated affair. The calumet was passed, and the sacred drink called *cassena*. The Indians made speeches, emphasizing the points by delivering belts of wampum, black on each edge and white in the middle. The design was intended to express peace, and that the path was fair and open. In the centre of these belts was the figure of a diamond, representing the council fire. The orator took one end of his belt and Boone held the other, while the Indian moved his forefinger down the rows of beads as he made his points. The braves sitting about waved ceremonial fans of eagle feathers. You may be sure that Boone and his companions prolonged this pow-wow as much as they were able. It was sundown before the last clause was agreed upon. This gave the garrison another night's respite, for it has never been the Indian custom to conclude an agreement the same day it was made. The white men played their points well, and appeared to be completely fooled. De Quindre was in high feather.

The commissioners went back to the fort with the understanding that they were to return the next morning for the purpose of signing. Both parties were insincere; and yet each hoped the other might go through with it. From the settlers' point of view it was worth trying, anyway; and as we have seen, the Frenchman had high anticipations.

Nevertheless, that night a strong body of Indians sneaked in and hid in the woods and bushes near the hollow, and the next morning when Blackfish led his party to the council trees, the settlers noted that many of the older men in his party had been replaced by strong young warriors. Boone mentioned this fact a little sardonically; but Blackfish looked him in the eyes and coldly declared that the party had not been changed. The Indians had come in white paint with swansdown on their heads, as though for genuine peace. After some more delay the "treaty" was signed. Blackfish said that it must now be confirmed by the representatives of his people or it could not have effect; and he called upon his retinue to step forward to shake the white man's hand. Now, strangely enough, it happened that there were eighteen men in Blackfish's retinue, just two to each white man, and at this they stepped forward, smiling affably, and seized the pioneers' hands. One, a little too eager, grasped too tightly and too soon, and betrayed the purpose by a movement toward the brush. Here showed Boone's judgment in his selection of his men. Old at Indian wiles, suspicious and alert, quick and strong, expert at wrestlers' tricks, they tripped their would-be captors, butted them, kicked them, wrenched themselves free and sprang aside. A hat waved and instantly from the bastion came the answering crack of rifles.

Boone and his comrades made their way to the fort under a storm of bullets, dodging from stump to stump, from hollow to hollow, from one hummock to another. So hot was the fire that one man had to lie out behind cover until the fall of night gave him a chance to leave his shelter. But if he was under the constant menace of the enemy, he was also under the protecting fire of his friends, and he escaped unscathed. Squire Boone was the only unlucky one. He received a bullet in the left shoulder.

But once the gates had clanged shut, the firing died. The anxious listeners within the fort could hear from within the forest the sounds of a great bustling to and fro: they heard horses being gathered in and loud commands that indicated the loading and packing of the ponies. Evidently the Shawnees were disgusted with the outcome of the negotiations and were getting ready to leave. The next morning just before daybreak the enemy noisily withdrew. The splashing of the horses could be heard as they crossed the river; commands could again be clearly distinguished; and fainter and fainter sounded the calls of De Quindre's bugle in the hills. Some of the younger men within the fort believed the trouble over, and wanted to open the gates and take the cattle forth, but Boone only laughed.

"Gone?" he answered them, "all but a few that took the

horses across are hidden right now within a hundred yards.
And most of those with the horses are back by now."

"Why are you so sure?" demanded one of the defenders,
struck by the Scout's certainty.

"Too much noise," said Boone; "an Indian does not make
noise. Did you hear the commands? They were too loudly
given—so we could hear."

So as a consequence the fort remained closed and the only
signs of life were, as before, the slow curling of smoke from
the chimneys. The calm lasted barely an hour. Then
from every stump and bush and tree came a stream of bullets from the impatient and chagrined savages, who were,
as Boone had stated, concealed everywhere within easy
range. The siege was on in earnest. Never before had
ammunition been used as lavishly. The British had issued
it in practically unlimited quantities to their new savage
allies; the forty packhorses furnished plenty of transportation. No longer did the invading party have to husband
its powder and lead, dependent on what it could itself carry.
A fierce and withering fire was every moment directed
against every loophole, every crack, that might even once
in a thousand times let a bullet through. The deep gorge
of the Kentucky River threw back the echoes in an almost
continual roll of thunder. The settlers had the greatest
difficulty in replying to this continuous leaden hail, for even
a momentary appearance at a porthole was attended by
great danger. Nevertheless, they managed so successfully
as to hold the savages within the fringe of woods. No shot

was wasted by these cool and practised men in miscellaneous firing. They had to see a mark before they pulled trigger.

But that very first day a sharp-eyed youth came to Boone with the information that a muddy streak had just begun to float down the river current; and as there had never been a muddy streak there before, he thought it worth reporting. After some exposure and a great deal of risk Boone caught sight over the cliff of a pole moving as though to loosen dirt.

"Some of the Frenchman's ideas," was his conclusion. "No Indian would have thought of that. They are starting a tunnel toward us and throwing the dirt into the river. They intend to mine us."

It was necessary to determine this certainly, as soon as possible. Under Boone's direction a rough but thick and bullet-proof breastwork or watch tower was pushed up, log by log, atop the blockhouse nearest the suspected work. From it the watchers could see the fresh earth as it was cast into the stream. The watch tower was strengthened, and from that time on, day and night, it was occupied by one or two riflemen who watched with ready weapons for a chance at this new danger.

There was only one thing to do. Just inside the walls, opposite the projected mine, a detail was set to work to dig a deep trench which should cut off the underground passage. It passed through several of the cabins that helped form the wall of the fort, and was about three feet wide and of great depth. It represented incredible labour on the part of men already wearied by their turn at the walls.

There was not a moment's respite, day or night. Black-fish divided his men into two parties who stood watch and watch, so that the battle was continuous. Within the fort there were no men to spare, so twenty-four hours each day the gaunt and haggard men clung to the portholes, snatching sleep a few minutes at a time. Luckily within a day or so a spell of foggy, drizzly weather set in. As the summer sun had beat fiercely down, this was very grateful. And especially was it providential in that it postponed for a little the Indians' plans for burning out the garrison.

Everybody within the fort expected that this siege would be like every other Indian siege so far known: that it would last two or three days at the very most, and then that the fickle savages, discouraged, would withdraw. But day succeeded day, and the intensity of the attack did not flag. The water in the reservoirs began to run low; and especially were the cattle in danger of drought. The strain of sleeplessness, excitement, and the constant alertness began to tell. Every night through the trunks of the forest trees could be seen the gleams of the campfires, and the forms of the savages off duty taking their rest and ease; recuperating, while their comrades held the attack, for another go at it. Their hunters could be seen returning with game. It was borne in upon the besieged that here at last was a serious determination to stay by until the job was finished, and Boonesborough, which had so many times stood in the way of savage and of royal ambitions, should be wiped off the border. The sounds of digging could now be plainly heard; and while Boone ordered the earth from the countermine to be thrown ostentatiously over the palisades to show that the project was understood, this seemed to have no effect in discouraging the savages. The latter must have been strongly persuaded by De Quindre of the certainty of success, for they hate manual labour, and nobody before nor since has ever succeeded in making them do so much digging. The trench was all very well, but the most sickening uncertainty and anxiety held everyone's mind. It might be possible to explode a quantity of powder outside the walls to create a breach; or it might be deflected to blow in the postern gate; or a dozen other contingencies that would occur to men already wearied out by constant battling.

One marksman among the savages caused a great deal of trouble. He was possessed of a good rifle, and he had gained a position in a tree with limbs so peculiarly arranged that he was able to shoot with the smallest and briefest exposure. The elevation permitted him to fire down into the compound. Before his position was located he had done considerable damage, hitting one or two people, but especially killing the cattle huddled in the centre. Among the people he hit was Jemima Boone, now Mrs. Flanders Callaway. When the position of this marksman was finally located, Boone himself ascended to the tower. He had not long to wait. The man in the tree prepared himself for another shot, and in so doing he exposed the top of his head.

Boone instantly fired.   The hidden marksman, struck squarely in the middle of the forehead, fell from the tree like a squirrel.   He proved to be Pompey, the renegade negro.   It was a wonderful shot. near two hundred measured yards.

One of the favourite amusements of the Indians for the moment off duty was to gather in little groups safely out of range and jeer at and insult the garrison.   Colonel Callaway, who was then getting pretty old, and who disapproved thoroughly of Boone's "irregular" methods of defense, saw here a chance to do something according to the approved rules of warfare.   So, casting back in his knowledge of history, he made him a "cannon" in accordance with the earliest tradition, out of wood, banded together with strap iron.   When this wonderful contrivance was finished, it was mounted atop a blockhouse and loaded with musket balls.   Nobody but the worthy colonel had any faith in the contraption; but he touched it off boldly, while the others held back at a safe distance.   It went off all right, with a most satisfactory whang and whistle of the bullets, and an awe-inspiring cloud of white smoke.   The Indians uttered yells of terror, and fairly fell over backwards to get into the woods.   None appeared again in sight for a long time; and when they did it was at a greatly increased range.   The old man turned her loose again.   Once more the noise; once more the cloud of white smoke; but when the latter cleared away it was found that the noble cannon had wrecked herself.   She was a one-shot gun.   The Indians evidently suspected what had happened, for they repeatedly dared the garrison to "shoot the big gun again."

Now on the seventh night after the arrival of the Indians the defenders were subjected to the grand assault of which all this previous fighting had been but a preparation intended to wear them down. Suddenly when, it is reported, "such a movement was entirely unexpected," the Indians succeeded in lodging fire-bundles against the side of the stockade and in shooting blazing arrows to the roofs of the cabins on that side of the fort. Immediately they swept the place with bullets, concentrating in such a manner that no human being attempting to extinguish the flames could live for a moment. The arrowheads had been wrapped in flax looted from one of the outside cabins, and with the inner oily fibre of the shell-bark hickory, and therefore they burned fiercely. For the first time the lofty spirits of the defenders fell to despair. The water supply was so nearly exhausted that there was not enough to be of any avail. By the use of brooms, themselves inflammable, the arrows on the roofs might be coped with; though even then at the greatest risk; but there seemed no way of reaching the conflagration against the stockade. The flames were by now blazing high, and the ruddy light was reflecting on the distant trees of the forest, whence the pandemonium of yells and savage cries, and the constant rattle and roar of the firearms assaulted even the calm and silent cup of heaven. The white men did what they could. A young fellow, whose name I have not been able to trace, sprang upon the roof and worked coolly for some moments, fully exposed to a concentrated fire by the enemy. In that hail of bullets it did not seem possible that any one could live for even the fraction of a second. The logs were shot to splinters about his feet, his clothes were pierced in several places, but he was untouched. When he had finished his task he uttered a defiant yell and leaped down. His preservation appeared to be a miracle, and greatly impressed the superstitions of the savages.

But in the meantime the stockade itself blazed merrily, and there was nothing to be done about it. The fort at last seemed doomed, and the blackest despair seized even these stout hearts.

So busily had the attack and defense been conducted; so rapidly had exciting and absorbing events followed one another; so brightly had the flames burned; that neither side had noticed a change that had slowly been taking place out in the calm spaces beyond the influence of these fierce passions. The clear brilliant dome of heaven had veiled. The aloof stars had dimmed, then had withdrawn one by one until the arch of the firmament was black. A little wind had sighed through the forest, a wind from the south, that in happier time would have carried with it the scent of damp things and the sound of croak-frogs. The night drew down closer and closer above the treetops. The little wind grew. And then with a crash and a flash, as though the "big gun" had again spoken, the sudden torrential thunderstorm of summer hot weather broke. Instantly the roofs began to stream. The brilliance of the fires was dimmed, flickered, died to dull redness, went out. Complete darkness took possession; and shortly complete silence, except for the roar of falling rain and the tinkle and drip of running water.

The discouraged and disgusted Indians withdrew for the moment. Inside the fort the settlers, with thanksgiving in their hearts, hastened to reassure their damaged defenses and to catch in all sorts of vessels as much as possible of the precious fluid. "Boonesborough," as Ranck expresses it, "was saved by the skin of its teeth."

From this time forward the Indians seemed to pin all their hopes on the tunnel they were digging. Their persistency in the hated manual labour was remarkable. On their side the settlers continued to beat off the numerous smaller attacks, to reply to the continuous fire, and to attempt to the best of their ability to dig countermines that would have at least a chance of effectiveness. The tower was always occupied by the best marksmen alert to take snap shots at any warrior who exposed himself on his way to or from the tunnel and the camp. These men were old hunters, familiar with the Shawnee language, and they whiled away their time bantering with their enemies with what Ranck calls a "curious courtesy."

" 'What are you red rascals doing down there?' " he reports an old hunter as shouting.

" 'Digging,' would be the return yell, 'Blow you all to the devil soon. What you do?' "

" 'Oh,' would be the cheerful reply, 'we are digging to meet you, and intend to bury five hundred of you.' "

And as the terrible days and nights succeeded one another hopes faded as to the arrival of the reënforcements. The men from Holston should long since have arrived. The extending delay might well mean that they had not started, might not be coming at all; and reënforcement seemed the only hope. The savages had unending resources, and for once unending patience. The garrison had dwindling supplies, dwindling energies. Sooner or later they must succumb. At this exact period Ranck reports their condition as follows:

"The outlook was black indeed. It was raining, and the pent-up people could slake their thirst, but they were worn out by the labour, the heat, and incessant watching and by privations, for the long-drawn-out provisions were about exhausted, and though some of the miserably reduced livestock remained, the pioneers had already reached the starvation point."

The tunnel had by now approached so close to the works that those back of the walls could distinctly hear the click of the implements. It was very evident that the time was at hand and that that very night the culmination would be reached. Nothing remained to be done. In uncertainty and anxiety the harassed and weary little band must wait the dark hours that would at last bring the long-delayed rush of the enemy. And to complete, as they thought, the tragic circle of their bad luck, it began shortly to rain, and the rain increased to a storm. "The night was so dark," says Ranck, "that the keenest watchers had no chance, except the poor one the flashes of lightning gave, to detect an advance of the enemy above the ground, while the tumult of the pouring rain and wind-swept forest drowned all other sounds and favoured every movement of the mining force." Nobody could guess the form the attack was to take; though all knew it would come off that night. They might blow up the postern gate and then rush in; they might penetrate to the countermine and thus gain entrance; they might have some deeper plan. The men and women and children could only wait through the slow dark hours for the bloody work to begin. At every loophole stood a watcher, the rain streaming from his bronzed countenance, straining his eyes into the thick darkness, straining his ears against the roaring storm; seeing nothing, hearing nothing, relaxing only for brief moments to curse deeply and fervently the fact that out of all the days of the year this one should have brought so fatal a tumult of the elements.

Slowly the hours crept by, and still the attack delayed. The exhausted men did not dare leave their post for a single instant. Midnight passed. One by one the hours of the early morning filed by on lagging steps. The first faint streaks of dawn showed in the east. The gray daylight came. Incredulous the defenders stared at one another. Not only had there been no assault during the hours most favourable, but for the first time in the long siege the rifle fire had ceased. The men at the loopholes reported the whole force of savages in leisurely retreat.

This was an old stratagem and nobody was deceived. But shortly across the stump-dotted no-man's land two figures could be discerned approaching. The figures were soon identified as Simon Kenton and Montgomery who, as you remember, had stayed behind in the heart of the Indian country for the purpose of stealing horses or "getting a shot or so." For the past week they had been hovering back of the Indian forces awaiting a chance to slip through. Now they brought the astounding news that the besiegers were in truth withdrawing. It seemed incredible; but it was true.

On investigation, however, the cause was apparent. A great quantity of faggots, kindling, and heavier fuel had been accumulated, which was to have been used by means of the tunnel approach to pile up against the stockade. Success at the first attempt with fire had come so close that we cannot wonder the savages had every confidence that this more careful plan could not fail. But the heavy rain-storm, which the defenders had so vigorously and mistakenly cursed, had wet everything down so thoroughly that fire was out of the question. That would not have mattered: it would have meant merely a postponement; but the rain had even further fulfilled its rôle under Providence. By now the ground had become pretty thoroughly soaked. This last torrential downpour had finished the softening of the earth, and the tunnel had caved in!

Such a catastrophe was too much for the patience of the Indians, already strained to the breaking point. Do what De Quindre and the other white men could, they were unable to overcome the reaction of a fierce disgust. Every plan they had made had gone wrong. At every juncture, it seemed an especial miracle had saved the fort. Even the fact that the young hero who had worked among the blazing arrows on the roofs had not been hit by at least one of the hail of bullets that sang around him seemed to them a mark of especial protection by the Great Spirit. But when the result of so much and such unaccustomed manual labour was destroyed in an instant, they just suffered a revulsion of feeling and quit in disgust.

CHAPTER XVII

THE first thing that occurred after the raising of the siege was a regrettable act of prejudice. Old Colonel Callaway had throughout the conduct of the defense resented the fact that Boone and not himself was at the head of affairs. Boone had not the military rank, and by strict military etiquette he probably was not in command. The settlers, however, insisted that he should lead them; and their confidence in his ability was justified. But the Colonel resented it: and immediately the Indians departed he insisted on preferring court-martial charges against Boone, accusing him, among other things, of treachery in attempting negotiations at all. Nothing could dissuade him from this foolish step, so Boone appeared. He was promptly acquitted of all charges, and the formal title and rank of major was conferred upon him so that there could be no similar trouble in the future.

About a week later the Holston men, the long-expected reënforcements, arrived, and Boone felt that at last he could rejoin his family. The enemy was defeated. Indeed for a time after this the white men kept them very busy in their own country by small expeditions. The guides on these expeditions were Boone's salt-makers, most of whom had by now been ransomed or exchanged from British captivity, and who of course knew the country well.

"Never," says Boone himself, "did the Indians pursue so disastrous a policy as when they captured me and my salt boilers, and taught us, what we did not know before, the way to their towns and the geography of their country; for though at first our captivity was considered a great calamity to Kentucky, it resulted in the most signal benefits to the country."

He found his wife and children again settled in a small log cabin in the country of the Yadkin. His appearance was the first intimation they had that he was not dead; and you can imagine the rejoicing, and that for a little period even the great Scout was content to settle down in peace.

But soon his restless spirit stirred again. The enactment of new land laws had stimulated a great tide of migration over the Wilderness Road. George Rogers Clark had captured Kaskaskia and Vincennes; Colonel Bowman had raided into the Indian country even as far as Chillicothe, and, while beaten off, had nevertheless sensibly abated the

Indians' thirst for foreign raids. In this fight the chief, Blackfish, was killed. The Indian danger, while always present, was not as great. Robinson, of Kentucky, gives us a vivid picture:

"Through privations incredible and perils thick thousands of men, women, and children came in successive caravans, forming continuous streams of human beings, horses, cattle, and other domestic animals, all moving onward along a lonely and houseless path to a wild and cheerless land. Behold the men on foot with their trusty guns on their shoulders, driving stock and leading packhorses, and the women, some walking with pails on their heads, others riding with children in their laps, and other children swung in baskets on horses fastened to the tails of others going before; see them encamped at night expecting to be massacred by Indians; behold them in the month of December in that ever-memorable season of unprecedented cold called the 'hard winter,' travelling two or three miles a day, frequently in danger of being frozen, or killed by the falling horses on the icy and almost impassable trace."

Boone could not long stand inaction. In October he returned with his family to Boonesborough, at the head of a band of neighbours; and it is noteworthy that he had with him two small cannon, the first to be taken into the country. It is also noteworthy that one of his comrades was Abraham Lincoln, the grandfather of the great President. The Boones and the Lincolns had always been close friends—indeed had intermarried—and now the Lincolns were following the Hunter's advice and moving to the new land. This was in 1780.

And 1780 was known as the Hard Winter. For seventy-five years after, it is said, men counted time from it. It will be recalled that this was the year that the heroes of the Revolution, on the Atlantic seaboard, suffered so severely. The autumn was especially late and mild, but the middle of November brought a cold snap that lasted without interruption for months. The snow was extraordinarily deep, and heavy winds drifted it. Immigrant wagons were stalled and held until the spring thaws. The streams were solid. The snow on the ground was crusted, the trees were as though made of glass, the firewood had to be chopped from blocks of ice. The very animals perished of the extreme cold; cattle and hogs around the station, and even bears, buffalo, wolves, and wild turkeys were found frozen in the woods. Sometimes the starving wild animals would come up to the very gates of the fort, accompanying the domestic cattle.

This was bad enough, but in addition the settlers themselves were very hard up for food. During Boone's absence the Indian troubles had gone on. Colonel Bowman had made an incursion into the Indian country and suffered defeat. George Rogers Clark had had better luck, and had burned the Indian towns of Chillicothe and Piqua after a sharp battle. On the other side a British officer, Colonel Byrd, at the head of a large force and equipped with two small cannon, had started into Kentucky. The wooden forts could not stand against ordnance of that sort. Two of the lesser stockades were taken and their inhabitants massacred or carried off into captivity. Fortunately for the rest of the Kentucky strongholds Byrd could not control the savages, who scattered to their villages intent on reaping the glory of this success. And all summer long small raiding parties on both sides were slipping back and forth across the border, inflicting what damage they could. At Boonesborough Colonel Callaway and a number of others were killed within rifle shot of the walls. Everywhere the Indians penetrated, they had industriously destroyed the crops; so that at the end of summer little corn was harvested. So in addition to the severity of the weather we see these people facing starvation as well. "Such was the scarcity of food," Bogart tells us, "that a single johnny-cake would be divided into a dozen parts, and distributed around to the inmates to serve for two meals. Sixty dollars a bushel was given for corn." The people lived largely on wild game, which was lean, poor, and unpalatable. Boone and Harrod hunted all winter in the severest of the weather, making long trips into the wilderness. The only gleam of comfort in the whole situation was that the cold kept the savages at home.

The winter was further saddened for the Boones by a tragedy that had occurred in October. Daniel and his brother Edward went hunting in the direction of the Blue Licks. On the return journey they were ambushed in the thick forest. At the crack of their rifles Edward fell dead;

but Daniel, seeming still to have a charmed life, shot the savage who had killed his brother, and leaped aside into the underbrush untouched. The savages yelled and rushed forward. The momentary delay while they scalped the younger Boone gave the elder his needed start. Stopping only once to reload and shoot another pursuer, he ran for three miles, twisting and doubling in the dense and tangled wilderness; by which time the Scout, with his usual display of woodcraft and endurance, had succeeded in shaking off all his human foes. But the Indians possessed a "smell-hound," as the quaint old diction has it; and the animal followed inexorably on the white man's trail. Finally, the Scout was forced in his turn to ambush the dog, when his never-erring rifle did the rest. But few of his many losses and misfortunes seem to have hit the Pioneer as did this. It struck as close to his heart as had even the death of his son, and yet we see his philosophy unruffled; and his simple justice toward all men, both white and red, unembittered.

Nor were these misfortunes more than begun. After Virginia had declared the proceedings of Judge Henderson's land company null and void it naturally followed that the titles to the land he had given were not worth anything. The colony made laws by which it was intended that the original settlers would be able to repurchase the same land, and so get clear title. Unfortunately, the drafting of those laws was in the hands of lawyers, and they made the process so complicated, tied it up with so much red tape, and required so many different steps in what should have been a simple matter that even to-day the mere reading of them over makes your head reel. You can imagine the effect they would have had on rough and illiterate frontiersmen. They could make neither head nor tail of it all, and in their attempts to fulfil the law's requirements they naturally made mistakes. Of these technical mistakes sharpers took advantage, so that it is a fact that in most instances the men who had pioneered and fought for this land in the end found themselves without an acre of it.

But this spring, the first year the new law was in effect, several of the settlers raised about twenty thousand dollars and sent Boone out to Richmond to act as agent for them. With this he took every dollar he could raise of his own. In some manner that is not recorded he was robbed. The sympathy for the honest pioneer was almost universal, so that the Legislature of Virginia promptly voted him a thousand acres of land free of charge, but there were not lacking the usual evil minds that whispered carelessness or actual dishonesty. This drew from the very men who had entrusted him with their money, and who had lost all of it, a tribute so fine that it is worth quoting here. It is an extract from a letter by Thomas Hart, the principal loser:

"I observe what you say respecting our losses by Daniel Boone. I heard of the misfortune soon after it happened, but not of my being a partaker before now. I feel for the poor people, who, perhaps, are to lose even their preëmptions, but I must say I feel more for Boone. Much degenerated must the people of this age be, when amongst them are to be found men to censure and blast the reputation of a person so just and upright, and in whose breast is a seat of virtue too pure to admit of a thought so base and dishonourable. I have known Boone in time of old, when poverty and distress had him fast by the hand; and in those wretched circumstances I have ever found him of a noble and generous soul, despising everything mean; and, therefore, I will freely grant him a discharge for whatever sums of mine he might have been possessed of at the time."

While Boone was in Richmond he had an opportunity to call upon Hamilton who had been the Governor at Detroit during Boone's captivity, and who had there showed him such kindness. Now Hamilton was himself a prisoner, having been captured at Vincennes by George Rogers Clark.

The next two years were full of varied excitement. Boone went to Richmond as a legislator. There he was captured, with others, by Tarleton; but was paroled after a few days. The conditions of the parole probably prevented his serving again, for he returned to Kentucky, after visiting his friends and relatives in Pennsylvania. On his return to Boonesborough he moved his family to a point about five miles away. There he put up a stockade of his own. The place was called Boone's Station and there he took up his abode, making again a home in the wilderness.

CHAPTER XVIII

THE darkest and bloodiest years of Kentucky's history were now to follow. The earliest pioneers had maintained themselves, as we have seen, against tremendous odds, but never against a skilfully led concerted movement. The new immigrants had built themselves stockades here and there, and had established a rough sort of militia organization for mutual aid. Boone received the rank of lieutenant-colonel.

At Detroit, on the other hand, the British used their utmost influence to arouse the Indians. By means of promises, gifts and warnings as to the constantly rising tide of white immigration they called in the most distant tribes to the warpath. The hope they offered was based on prospects of success under a new policy of concerted action and no quarter given. They were the more excited to effort by the fact that on the Atlantic seaboard the tide of war had at last turned. The battles of King's Mountain and the Cowpens had been fought, and Yorktown was not long to wait. Now, if ever, the British must strike decisively, if they hoped to retain any of the rich domain of the West. And like desperate men they used desperate means. It is a blot on history, and gave birth to a slow-dying hatred. The Indians took the warpath everywhere; often led by white men more savage than themselves, such men as the Girtys and McKee, renegades from their own side, filled with hatred of their kind, and inspired by a relentless cruelty that had not even the Indian code of custom and honour to restrain it. Once more all the border was aflame, and the annals of the time are filled with raids, burnings, massacres, tortures, and captivities; with heroic defenses against odds; with hairbreadth escapes; with stratagem and bravery. At that not one tenth was ever told. The people were too busy with their bitter and desperate conflict for a foothold, for very existence, to have left any record of a heroism that became almost a daily commonplace to them. For the land hunger had bitten the vitals of the people, and in face of the horrors of savage warfare they were still pouring in.

They came over the Wilderness Road in hundreds. They floated in even greater numbers in flat boats down the Ohio. These flat boats were huge affairs, scow built, from twenty to sixty feet in length, broad of beam, unbelievably clumsy. The people embarked on them with all their goods, including their horses and domestic animals. As the demand greatly exceeded the supply, these craft were always crowded fully to the danger point, and away beyond the comfort point. They were handled by long sweeps, and must, of course, drift with the current. The whole duration of the voyage must be spent on board, for the banks of the river were always occupied by savages, following like vultures the slow progress of the flotilla, awaiting eagerly an opportunity for successful attack. If one of these scows swung in too close to either bank, if it lagged behind or ran ahead of its convoy, if it deviated for an instant from the narrow strip of mid-stream safety, it was fired at, pounced upon, its occupants massacred without mercy. The published accounts of such instances would fill many volumes the size of this.

It was, on the whole, good scalp-hunting for the Indians, never better. While many of these newcomers to the country were a hard-bitten, wary, experienced lot and could take care of themselves with the best, and while others employed old-time borderers to act as guides, a very large number had little or no experience with Indians. These often fell an easy prey.

Possibly the fact that scalp-hunting was so good went far toward preventing large concerted actions. The Indians would rather roam about in small parties, ambushing, killing and scalping; making isolated attacks on outlying cabins and small settlements, than gather in big formal armies for considered invasions. Indeed, it is recorded that in the summer of 1781 McKee, Brant, and a number of other

British leaders and Indian chiefs assembled an army of over a thousand braves for the purpose of opposing George Rogers Clark. Brant went off on a scout with about a hundred warriors and destroyed a party of white men utterly. The Indians were vastly pleased at this, and immediately wanted to quit the whole expedition and go home to brag about it. Then they heard that Clark had abandoned his project. The rumour was enough. In spite of the commanders' best efforts the Indians began at once to disband, some returning to their villages to celebrate their little victory, the rest scattering in all directions to do the individual raiding they loved. So that expedition dissolved.

In this manner, though the warfare was continuous and very deadly, it was more a series of individual combats and skirmishes than a settled campaign. For that reason the exciting stories of the time are almost without number. It would be impossible to tell a hundredth part of them; but here are a few samples, very briefly related. They are not especially noteworthy, as compared to the others.

At a small fort called Estill's Station twenty-five Indians by a sudden dash killed and scalped a young woman and carried off a negro slave. Estill and seventeen men at once rode in pursuit. They caught up with the marauders, who proved to be Wyandots, and at once engaged them. For two hours the fight lasted, the Indians refusing to give ground, and for some reason fighting stubbornly on in the face of heavy loss. At the end of that time there remained

AN HOUR'S WARNING

only six Indians and two white men! These withdrew by common consent.

At the "crab orchard" a woman, her children, and one negro happened to be alone in a cabin while the men were absent. Suddenly the door opened and a painted warrior slipped in. With the instant presence of mind of frontier children, the youngsters slammed and bolted the door behind him before others could enter. The woman, in a desperate fury, attacked the warrior with an axe and actually cut his head from his shoulders! After that the little garrison made so brave a defense that the raiding party withdrew.

In the Wyandot nation were seven warriors who hunted and made war together as a band. Four of them were brothers, and all of them were men of great stature and strength. They had made numberless raids into white territory, and had gradually become known and dreaded. Now in a settlement near the scene of one of these raids lived two brothers, Adam and Andrew Poe, equally famed for strength and skill; and they were two of the eight white men who took the Wyandots' trail. The pursuers, helped by the moon, managed to follow at night; and so by the following morning found themselves near the enemy. Andrew Poe thereupon turned off at a stream, intending to sneak up the bed and so get in the rear of the Indians. As he neared the stream he heard something; and creeping up cautiously he found himself looking down on two Indians whispering together. One of them Andrew recognized by his truly gigantic stature and bulk to be Bigfoot, the most renowned of the fighters. Andrew aimed at this chief; but his rifle missed fire. Before the startled Indians could move, Andrew leaped down on them from above. He landed on Bigfoot and knocked him down, and at the same movement got his arm around the smaller Indian's neck, so that all three of them rolled on the ground. For a moment or so Andrew managed to pin them down, but before he could get hold of his knife Bigfoot wrapped his arms tightly about him and shouted to the other Indian to run for his tomahawk, which had been spilled on the shore a few feet away. Andrew immediately discovered that the chief was too powerful for him, so he ceased to struggle; but he kept his eye on the other Indian, and as the latter ran up with the tomahawk Andrew kicked him so hard in the chest as to knock the tomahawk out of his hand and send him staggering. He recovered immediately both his health and his tomahawk and again approached. This time he struck, but Andrew wriggled enough to take the blow on his arm instead of his head. The wound was a deep one, but it did not appear to disable him. He put forth all his strength and wrenched himself free. With the agility of a panther he sprang to where a loaded rifle lay on the sand, snatched it up, and shot the smaller Indian: but was immediately seized again by the giant and hauled to the ground. Instantly the two were locked together in a furious hand-to-hand struggle. They had no weapons, as each had lost both his knife and tomahawk. Andrew was the smaller man, but he had great skill in wrestling and boxing so the contest was now not so uneven as it looked. Over and over they fought on the sands of the shore, sometimes one on top, sometimes the other, until they rolled into the river. Andrew caught the chief by the scalp lock and held him under water. Fainter grew his struggles; at last they ceased. Andrew relaxed his hold. Instantly the Indian was on his feet and rushing on his enemy. He had been pretending dead, "playing possum." The enemies floundered into deep water, and there they drew apart and struck out for the shore. Here the Indian excelled, and Andrew was outdistanced. The chief struck shallow water and ran up the sands to seize the rifle. Andrew at once turned to swim out into the stream, keeping an eye on the chief, and hoping to escape the shot by diving.

While Andrew Poe was in all this various tribulation, his brother and the other six white men had run across the rest of the Indians. They discovered each other at the same instant. A fierce combat took place. Three of the white men and four Indians were killed, and the solitary surviving Wyandot escaped badly wounded. From this bloody fight Adam emerged unhurt, and at once went in search of his brother in the direction from which the sound of a shot had come, that with which Andrew had killed the smaller Indian. Adam came out on the bank above the river at the precise moment that Andrew had turned to swim away, and the chief had seized the empty rifle from the sands. Andrew was covered with blood and unrecognizable. Adam thought him an Indian and fired at him, hitting him in the shoulder, and hardly had he pulled trigger when he saw the chief.

The white man and the Wyandot faced each other with empty guns. The Indian grinned.

"Who load first, shoot first," he challenged.

The men dropped the butts of their rifles to the ground. It became a very pretty race as to which could beat the other in loading. The chief was expert, and was well ahead in this novel contest up to the moment when he attempted to use his ramrod. It slipped through his fingers and fell into the stream. With the cool judgment of the practised warrior he knew he had lost, and with the fortitude of a savage he accepted his fate calmly. Letting fall his piece on the sands he tore open the front of his shirt to expose his breast, and fell with the ball through his heart. Andrew was then rescued by his brother.

A very remarkable episode mentioned by all the writers in that time occurred after a successful attack on one of the flat boats we mentioned a time back. The massacre was pretty complete, but two men managed to escape notice and hide out until the Indians had gone. Then by great good luck they discovered one another: for one of them had both arms broken, and the other both legs!

"Well," said one of them cheerfully, "we've got all the arms and legs we need between us." And they started out methodically to supply each other's deficiencies. For some weeks they lived near the battlefield. The man who had his legs did all the walking: he pushed firewood over to his friend; he made long cautious circuits and drove game in; he carried the other pickaback when it became absolutely necessary to use a pair of hands at a distance. The other man built the fire, did the cooking, fed his companion, shot the game driven toward him. A flat boat picked them up eventually.

Another of these flat-boat massacres took place when a great many Indians cut off several boats from a convoy. All but one of those so cut off were captured and their occupants killed; but one, under command of an old sea captain, put up a desperate defense from behind the frail bulwarks. One by one the men were killed or wounded; the horses and cattle aboard were panic stricken; the women and children huddled low, not knowing from one second to another whether they would be trampled to death, would receive a bullet, or would see painted forms leaping over the gunwale. Indeed twice the Indians did come to close grips and were only beaten off by the most desperate fighting. At last the attack was withdrawn and the wounded could be cared for, the dead animals removed, and the slain white people prepared for burial. It was a sad task and a long task; but at length it was finished, and the shattered little band floated in some semblance of order down the stream. Then up spoke a boy of eleven years who had sat huddled out of the way at one end of the boat.

"Captain," he said, "will you see what you can do for my head?"

The captain looked. A bullet, probably spent from passing through the planks, had lodged under the skin of the boy's forehead. Carefully the seaman cut it out. The boy did not wince.

"Now, captain," he begged as the other turned away, "will you look at my arm."

It turned out that the elbow had been broken by a shot. Before the arm was bound up the captain was forced to remove a piece of bone.

"There, my lad," said he when the operation was finished, "But why didn't you sing out?"

"You ordered us to lie down and make no noise," replied the boy, "and," he added quaintly, "there was noise enough without mine."

In an outlying cabin lived a settler named Bingaman. The cabin had one room below, and a loft. Below slept Bingaman, his wife and child and his old mother. In the loft was a hired man. Late one night the inmates were awakened by a terrific crash on the door. Eight Indians had assailed the cabin, and had run at the door with a log of wood as a battering ram. Bingaman had just time to leap from the bed and seize his rifle when the door gave way. Instantly he discharged the piece at the dark figures in the doorway. Four or five streaks of fire answered him. He swept the two women and the child under the bed and clubbing his long heavy rifle, leaped single-handed against the foe.   The door had swung to and the room was in absolute darkness.   Like a madman Bingaman laid about him.   Several times he was grappled and borne down, but each time his wiry strength enabled him to shake himself free.   One after another his foes were killed or crippled by his powerful blows until at last but one remained; and this one fled terror-stricken.   When a light was struck the place looked like a shambles.   The women and the child crept forth from under the bed. Bingaman then discovered that at the first fire his wife had been wounded in the breast.   At that it took the combined persuasions of all three to prevent his going up in the loft to kill the hired man, who had prudently kept out of it.

But we have not the space to multiply instances.   It is stated that in these years fifteen hundred white people were massacred in Kentucky.

CHAPTER XIX

THESE troubles came to a climax in July of 1782. Two British officers, Captains Caldwell and Mc-Kee, started from Detroit in command of over a thousand Indians, a tremendous army for those days. This great force was to settle the matter once and for all; crush the feeble and scattered forts; massacre the inhabitants, already exhausted by the long struggle; and so assure the vast country west of the Allegheny for the crown. It was by far the largest body of men, either white or red, ever gotten together west of the mountains. It had every prospect of success, but the expedition fizzled out, as so many had done before it, because of the inability of Indians in large bodies to "carry through." They were no sooner well started than somebody came into camp with the rumour that George Rogers Clark intended to attack the Shawnee villages. That was enough. Clark's determined mid-winter march against Vincennes had impressed the Indians with the idea that nothing was impossible to him. In vain did Caldwell and McKee appeal to their reason and commonsense. It did no good to ask whence Clark had obtained his men, how he was going to get to the Shawnee villages; the red men remembered distinctly that in the dead of winter, and apparently from the middle of an overflowed flood of ice water, Clark had once materialized out of the thin air. They turned around and scuttled back to see about those precious villages.

Of course the rumour was entirely groundless, but that did the harassed Britons little good. Once the savages had retasted the delights of home life and stewed fresh corn they hated to arouse themselves for the second time to face the discomforts and dangers of the war trail. After trying without avail to rekindle the spark of enterprise McKee and Caldwell had to set out again with only three hundred instead of the thousand. The reason they retained three hundred was because these faithful adherents were not Shawnees, but Hurons and lake tribes, and so still far from home. Three hundred was even yet a formidable force but it was not a crushing force. They crossed the Ohio and at once proceeded to attack one of the small stockaded forts, called Bryan's or Bryant's Station. This was the northernmost, and if the Indians could take it by surprise, the four other stations north of the Kentucky River should fall an easy prey. The over-eagerness of some of the younger Indian spies betrayed them to the white scouts, who managed to get a warning to the garrison. Now occurred the heroic deed before narrated when under the eyes of the savages the women and children went to the spring to bring in a supply of water. Hardly were they within the walls of the fort, however, when the Indians perceived that their presence was known; perhaps by the slamming shut of the big gate. At any rate, they attacked so suddenly that one or two white men, who had lingered in the cornfields just outside, were killed.

At first but a small body of the Indians manifested themselves. They appeared at a safe distance, yelling and prancing about, hurling defiance at the fort, hoping to decoy the whites into the open, or at least to attract all attention to that side of the fort in order to give a chance for the real rush on the other. But these seasoned old Indian fighters were not deceived. A dozen of the youngest and most active men were slipped out through the gate and instructed to make a lot of noise and carry on a mock combat with the decoy band of Indians. In the meantime, the defenders silently gathered behind the walls on the other side of the fort.

Sure enough, hardly had the young men begun to bang away and yell, when a vast horde of Indian warriors rushed the walls from the other side. The long Kentucky rifles spoke with deadly accuracy. The attack withered back discouraged, and the young men on the other side, laughing heartily, and mocking the decoys, slipped back through the gate. At once the Indians surrounded the whole fort, each creeping up as close as he could find shelter; and opening fire in the usual Indian fashion. This kept up for several hours

The white men had sent out their swiftest runners, when first the news of Indians was brought, to seek aid at the other stations. By luck one of these came across a force of men from Lexington out with the intention of cutting off the retreat of marauding savages across the Kentucky. Nobody seems to have had the slightest idea that the red men were out in such force. The scouts must have encountered only small advance parties. Major Todd and forty men were detached from the main body to rescue the fort! Seventeen of these were on horseback: the rest on foot.

There is no question that this little band would have been killed to the last man had it not been that the Indians were completely surprised by their appearance. Evidently they had not expected any one from the outside for some time yet. Todd and his men came toward the fort by a road that led through a field of corn taller than a man; and were right among the Indians before they were seen. A few startled warriors fired upon them. Todd and the horsemen struck spurs to their horses and riding hard reached the fort. The footmen doubled back and disappeared in the dense forest before the foe recovered his wits. One of these, however, was killed, and three wounded.

A few years before this time the situation of the fort would have been even more desperate than was that of Boonesborough in its memorable siege. But Boonesborough stood alone in a wilderness, while now, within reasonable distance, were many settlements from which reënforcements would shortly come. The Indians and their white allies understood this perfectly. All that night the little garrison were subjected to one ferocious attack upon another, with the usual shooting of blazing arrows, rushing of the stockade with flaring torches. The defenders managed by terrific effort to maintain the walls, and the day broke with the fort still safe.

Our old acquaintance, Simon Girty, was with the invaders, and at one time tried to scare the garrison into surrender by tall talk of artillery. Of course you can readily see that even one small iron cannon would have changed utterly all this backwoods warfare. No stockade could have stood for a moment. Therefore artillery was the one thing dreaded. Heretofore the distance such a weapon would have to be dragged through a rough and unbroken wilderness had made its use impossible. But the dread was always there. However, nobody was particularly scared. A young fellow with a ready tongue, named Reynolds, happened to be in the garrison. He leaped to the parapet in full view.

"You ask if we do not know you?" he shouted. "Know you! Yes. We know you too well. Know Simon Girty! Yes. He is the renegade, cowardly villain, who loves to murder women and children, especially those of his own people. Know Simon Girty! Yes. His father was a panther and his dam a wolf. I have a worthless dog that kills lambs. Instead of shooting him I have named him Simon Girty. You expect cannon, do you? Cowardly wretches like you would not dare touch them off if you had them. Even if you could batter down our pickets I, for one, hold your people in too much contempt to discharge rifles at them. I have been roasting a number of hickory switches with which we mean to whip your cutthroats out of the country."

With a laugh he jumped down out of sight just in time to escape a hundred or so of exasperated bullets.

However, the Indians knew that Reynolds spoke the truth in one particular. They were aware that the riflemen of the other settlements must be assembling, and would shortly descend upon them. The first attack having failed, they had shot their bolt. On the morning of the seventeenth of August they withdrew, very angry over the failure.

Before going on with the main narrative, it will be amusing for us to learn what further we can of this same young fellow, Reynolds, with the "ready tongue," for later we shall meet him at the disastrous battle of Blue Licks. His tongue evidently was always rather too ready. We encounter him in the militia command of a Captain Patterson, described as good-hearted and active, but a "very profane swearing man." The latter description must have been mild, for at the end of four days Captain Patterson decided either to make him modify his swearing or send him home. Of course we do not know how religious a man Patterson was; but the backwoods leaders of those days were not notably squeamish. The captain waited until Reynolds was in full swing, and then called him down hard and publicly. Temporary effect. Next day the "profane swearing man" was at it as bad as ever. This time Patterson enforced military discipline not only by an even severer scolding, but by a promise of a bottle of rum if he "immediately quit his profanity and swearing." Four days later, when the expedition had ended, Reynolds demanded his quart. Captain Patterson ventured to doubt whether the young man had gone four full days without a single oath. Reynolds appealed to the company then drawn up at parade. To a man they said they had not heard Reynolds "cuss a solitary cuss" since he had been rebuked. "Then," says the chronicler, "the spirits were drank."

To the fort at Bryan's Station gathered the riflemen summoned to its aid. Boone was one of the first, with his neighbours and his son Frank. They were the best type of the backwoods fighters, these men, but unruly, undisciplined, headlong, and impatient of control. Their leaders persuaded rather than commanded them. And owing to the fact that they had gathered from many communities there was really no one man who could so command them all. They were angry and eager for vengeance; and they were exultant over the repulse of the Indians by the fort. Next day they set forth, one hundred and eighty-two of them, all on horseback, all armed with the long rifle. It was known that the County Lieutenant, Logan, was raising a large body of men in haste, and would soon be on the scene; but those already on the spot feared to await his arrival lest the enemy scatter and escape.

CHAPTER XX

THE invading band had retreated in a leisurely fashion, following the wide, hard-beaten buffalo roads that led to the Blue Licks. By afternoon the pursuers had come to where their enemies had camped the night before. Boone and the other leaders examined the indications carefully, and easily determined that they were badly outnumbered. However, they continued the pursuit, and early the following morning came to the Blue Licks.

As they drew near, a number of scattered Indians could plainly be seen climbing up the rocky ridge on the other side of the river. You can imagine how this sight excited the hotheads in the party. However, in spite of the impatience of the latter, the older men halted and called a council. Boone, as the most noted Indian fighter, was asked for his opinion and advice.

"We have followed them too easily," he told his companions; "the trail has been too plain. It has been made plain purposely. Without doubt the Indians know that we are an inferior force and they want to be followed and attacked. They have marked their trail too plainly, I tell you; they have left their campfires burning; and there have been too few campfires for the other indications of the numbers. They are trying to make. us believe they are fewer than they are. It has been all right for us to press them hard in a hasty pursuit, otherwise they might have scattered. My advice is to wait now for Logan."

The responsible men, including the leaders, Todd and Trigg, agreed to this; but the younger men, under the instigation of a rash fool named Hugh McGarry, raised a storm of protest.

"If we are to attack," then said Boone, "let us divide into two parties, one to cross the river in front and the other to go around the bend of the river and strike the rear."

"And in the meantime, the red varmints get away!" shouted McGarry, with a furious gesture toward the handful of savages temptingly exposed on the face of the rocks, as they made their slow way upward.

"At least send ahead scouts!" cried Boone in desperation.

But McGarry, raising the warwhoop, spurred into the river, brandishing his rifle.

"All who are not cowards follow me!" he yelled.

Instantly the wild young fellows, carried away by the excitement of the moment, dashed in after him, crossing the stream in huddlement and confusion.

Nothing remained but to follow and to save the day if possible. Todd and Trigg took the centre and right of the line respectively, while Boone and his own men hastened to the left. Almost immediately the blunderers fell into the ambush. Boone won his fight on his own side of the line, pushing the enemy back steadily and inflicting about all the loss that enemy was to sustain. But the rest of the line was simply overwhelmed. Painted warriors arose on all sides of the trap into which headstrong folly had led their foes, and poured in a withering fire. Todd, Trigg, and Harlan, the three leaders, were almost immediately killed. A wild riot followed. Everyone rushed back toward the ford, the pursuing Indians at their heels; indeed, fairly among them. Boone's little force on the left, without support, found itself abandoned. Surrounded on three sides by increasing numbers, it, too, broke back toward the river. It is recorded that Boone himself was the last to leave the field. As he drew back his son Frank fell. The old hunter turned like a lion at bay, beat off his pressing enemies, with an effort heaved the body across his shoulders to save it from the scalping knife. As he staggered toward the river a gigantic Indian rushed upon him, tomahawk uplifted. With a groan Boone dropped the body of his son, shot the Indian through the heart, and then, as his enemies closed, leaped away.

Every inch of this country was known to him. He broke through his pursuers to one side, darted down a little ravine known only to himself, outran several Indians, and finally made his way back to Bryan's Station by a widely circuitous route.

One of Boone's staunchest supporters in the preliminary councils had been a man named Netherland. Indeed so vehement had he been that the younger men had laughed him to scorn as a coward. Now in the headlong retreat he led the way and was the first to recross the river. We can imagine some of his companions, even in the turmoil of this disaster, sparing him a contemptuous thought. However, he proved to be one of the few sensible men present, and one with the truest courage. No sooner had he gained the south bank when he pulled in his horse and dismounted, calling loudly on his comrades to make a stand there to cover the flight. Almost all within sound of his voice obeyed him. They opened a steady, well-directed fire on the pursuers. At that moment the ford was jammed with horsemen, footmen, and Indians. Netherland's vigorous fire forced the latter back long enough to permit the confusion to straighten itself out a little. On the south bank the white men began to defend themselves and, in small groups, to retreat slowly.

Now among the participants in this battle were both that "profane swearing man," Aaron Reynolds, and his old commander with whom he had clashed on the occasion which happily culminated when the "spirits were drank." When the rout began Captain Patterson could not find his horse, and as he was still suffering from unhealed wounds inflicted in another Indian fight, the hasty flight afoot soon exhausted him. Just as he gave up all hope young Reynolds leaped his horse over intervening obstacles to his side; dismounted; and, without a by-your-leave, bundled the captain into the saddle. Before Patterson realized what was going on, he was dashing into the river. He was actually the last man to cross. Some of the Indians were running alongside shooting at him, but he escaped without another scratch.

In the meantime, Reynolds, who was a remarkably strong and active young fellow, ran and dodged and reached the river safely, but not at the ford. He was forced to plunge in and swim across. On the other side, after outdistancing his pursuers, he stopped to wring out his buckskin trousers. Those of you who have worn buckskin will appreciate the necessity for that. When wet, buckskin is heavy, clammy, and stretches absurdly, so that the garment which when dry is decidedly too small, when wet has enough material in it to furnish out two grown men and a boy. Just as he was pulling off the trousers, and so was all tangled up, two Indians pounced on him and took him prisoner. But Reynolds was not at the end of his resources. Watching his chance he knocked down one of his captors and escaped. Later he met Patterson who, of course, thanked him earnestly; at the same time asking rather curiously why he had taken such desperate chances for the sake of a man with whom he had had nothing but trouble and difficulty. He replied that ever since Patterson had made him stop swearing he had felt a strong affection for him and had completely reformed not only his actions but his ways of thinking. To round out the story, Patterson then gave him a horse and saddle and "a hundred acres of prime land." This was the first real property the young man had ever owned. It—and his narrow escape—steadied him. He settled down, and eventually became a strong and devout church member.

Two days later Logan came up with his four hundred men. The combined forces returned to the battlefield, but there remained nothing to do but bury the dead.

The loss to the backwoodsmen was very heavy. Of the one hundred and eighty-two, seventy were killed outright; besides the wounded, and seven men captured. Of the latter, four, as was customary, were put to torture. One man was spared because of his strength, activity, and daring. In running the gauntlet he managed by great exertion and speed almost to gain the council house, when he darted one side, threw one Indian violently to the ground, thrust his head between the legs of another and tossed him over his back, so gaining the clear. Then, instead of running away, he leaped on a stump, knocked his heels together, flopped his arms, and crowed like a rooster. It tickled the Indians so much that one of the older chiefs adopted him on the spot.

This crushing defeat plunged all the border in mourning. Hardly a cabin but had lost one of its menfolk. For a time the country lay supine. The Indians, satiated with victory, had disappeared into the gloom of the northern forests. In the next few months small bands of them made frequent raids, striking terror, keeping fresh the feeling of disaster. Boone and others wrote many times and indignantly to the Virginia Legislature complaining of the lack of protection and aid. At last George Rogers Clark took the matter in hand. He sent out runners in all directions summoning all fighting men to gather for the purpose of inflicting on the Indians a decisive blow. It was the psychological moment. Wearied by repeated attack without the chance of striking back, the frontier arose eagerly. Every man who could pull trigger hastened to the meeting place, and with him brought all the cattle, packhorses, and supplies he could obtain. On the 4th of November Clark crossed the Ohio at the head of one thousand and fifty mounted men; a huge army for the backwoods. They captured and burned many of the Indian villages; defeated McKee, one of the British officers who had led the invading force; and, what was of most importance, destroyed great quantities of corn and other provisions.

The blow was a heavy one in itself, but particularly it disheartened the Indians because they had thought the battle of Blue Licks must utterly have crushed the white man. This did not look much like it. The white man was apparently stronger than ever. If such a disaster as the Blue Licks defeat could not check him, then nothing could. The Indians were completely discouraged. Although for some years longer Kentucky was here and there subjected to many raids, never again did the savages attack in force or with a serious purpose.

CHAPTER XXI

IN THIS period Daniel Boone was still called upon to fill a part. He was both sheriff and county lieutenant, and his duties led him often far afield in pursuit of, or scouting after, small marauding bands of Indians. Between times he was often required to act as guide or surveyor for men searching out desirable tracts of land for speculation or settlement; or as pilot to one or another of the parties of immigrants coming in over the Wilderness Road; or as hunter to supply wild meat to this or the other body of persons; or to furnish armed guards of riflemen against Indians. His fame spread. It was said that he was almost the best-known man in America, and that his renown had even extended to Europe.

Kentucky filled up rapidly. Over twelve thousand persons came into the country in 1783 and 1784. Almost over night the life was changing. There were more crops; and stores, and market places, and regular streets in some of the towns. Lawyers, doctors, traders, speculators came in. An export trade of Kentucky produce, such as bacon, beef, salt, ginseng, tobacco, sprang up both across the mountains and down the great waterways.

Boone, when at home, lived not far from Boonesborough on a farm. Among his Indian enemies his fame was as great as, or greater than, with the whites. Twice he had escaped from them in a mortifying fashion, after they had supposed him about to join them, and of course his now innumerable exploits in war against them had gained him reputation and respect. To capture him would be a great feat; and the attempt was frequently made. Boone continued to lead a life of danger and escape.

One such episode he himself tells. It seems that among other things Boone raised tobacco. Here is the account of the adventure as reported by Peck, the man to whom Boone narrated it:

"As a shelter for curing the tobacco he had built an enclosure of rails a dozen feet in height and covered with cane and grass. Stalks of tobacco are generally split and strung on sticks about four feet in length. The ends of these are laid on poles placed across the tobacco house, and in tiers, one above the other, to the roof. Boone had fixed his temporary shelter in such a manner as to have three tiers. He had covered the lower tier and the tobacco had become dry, when he entered the shelter for the purpose of removing the sticks to the upper tier, preparatory to gathering the remainder of the crop. He had hoisted up the sticks from the lower to the second tier, and was standing on the poles which supported it, while raising the sticks to the upper tier, when four stout Indians with guns entered the low door and called him by name.

"'Now, Boone, we got you. You no get away more. We carry you off to Chillicothe this time. You no cheat us any more.'

"Boone looked down on their upturned faces, saw their loaded guns pointed at his breast, and recognizing some of his old friends the Shawnees who had made him prisoner near Blue Licks in 1778, coolly and pleasantly responded:

"'Ah, my old friends, glad to see you.'

"Perceiving that they manifested impatience to have him come down, he told them he was quite willing to go with them, and only begged that they would wait where they were, and watch him closely, until he could finish removing the tobacco.

"While thus parleying with them, Boone inquired earnestly respecting his old friends in Chillicothe. He continued for some time to divert the attention of these simple-minded men by allusions to past events with which they were familiar, and by talking of his tobacco, his mode of curing it, and promising them an abundant supply. With their guns in their hands, however, they stood at the door of the shed, grouped closely together so as to render his escape apparently impossible. In the meantime, Boone carefully gathered his arms full of the long, dry tobacco leaves, filled with pungent dust, which would be as blinding and stifling as the most powerful snuff, and then with a leap from his station twelve feet high, came directly upon their heads, filling their eyes and nostrils and so bewildering and disabling them for the moment that they lost all self-possession and control.

"Colonel Boone related this adventure with great glee, imitating the gestures of the bewildered Indians. He said that notwithstanding his narrow escape, he could not resist the temptation, as he reached the door of his cabin, to look around to witness the effect of his achievement. The Indians, coughing, sneezing, blinded, and almost suffocated by the tobacco dust, were throwing out their arms and groping about in all directions, cursing him for a rogue and calling themselves fools."

It is written in the histories that from a thousand to fifteen hundred people were killed by Indians during these years. The big formal invasions were over. The Indians realized that they could not hope to drive the white man from the land. Nevertheless, the lone settler's cabin, the incautious immigrant train, the inexperienced newcomer from the eastern civilizations offered tempting opportunities for obtaining coveted scalps. It was an uneasy time, full of adventure. We have not space to detail even a small percentage of the exciting stories that have been preserved to us. It was said that reaching Kentucky by flat boat on the river was like running the gauntlet. "For a long time," says Abbott, "it had been unsafe for any individual, or even small parties, unless very thoroughly armed, to wander beyond the protection of the forts." You may be sure the white men were not idle, nor did they suffer without attempts at retaliation. Indeed so many Indians were captured that Boone called a great council at Maysville, the small station near which he lived, to discuss an exchange of prisoners. This was arranged. As usual, the impression made by Boone was so strong that the Indian chiefs voluntarily issued orders to their people that in the future, if any people of Maysville were captured, they were to be treated kindly and with the deepest respect. Nor was this an idle bluff. Some time after someone from Maysville *was* captured, and did receive the most extraordinary good treatment.

But now Boone was to receive an unmerited blow, a blow that not only hit at his material prosperity, but which hurt his feelings, embittered him against civilization, and almost embittered him against his fellowman. Almost, I say; for the gentle, friendly character of the old pioneer was proof against even the shock of essential injustice and ingratitude. However he might resent and despise the institutions of men, he seems never to have lost his kindly feeling for men themselves.

With the influx of new settlers had come stable government and the formal laws and regulations that belong with it.   Among these were of course laws as to the ownership of land.   Certain formalities had to be complied with, as was quite just and proper; but these formalities were often so framed as to favour land sharps and speculators, which was not right and proper at all.   One morning the sheriff knocked at Boone's door.   To his hurt astonishment he found that his title to his own home had been questioned in the courts.   Some technicality he had not fulfilled of the many made necessary by the legislation of men who had lately come to the country.

The old pioneer was astounded.   That he who had opened this vast area to white settlement, millions of acres of it, should be questioned in the ownership of the few he had selected for his own use, seemed to him incredibly unjust. And it was unjust.   There is no doubt that technically he did not possess clear title: there is also no doubt that morally he had the clearest title possible.   The unscrupulous skunks in human form who saw their chance to put in a legally sound claim in opposition, who could contemplate for a moment ousting a man of Boone's character and history; the lawyers who prosecuted the case; the rigid-minded judges who could see no possible course of action other than that laid down; the legislature that did not, if necessary, pass especial laws assuring his ownership; the supine public opinion that did not rise in indignation over such an outrage, are almost equally to blame.   That sort of legal argument to excuse injustice can command the patience of no sensible man.   Shortly, after a series of lawsuits, the old woodsman found himself without a single acre in the land he had discovered and subdued!

"My footsteps have often been marked with blood," said he. "Two darling sons and a brother have I lost by savage hands, which have also taken from me forty valuable horses and an abundance of cattle. Many dark and sleepless nights have I been a companion for owls, separated from the cheerful society of men, scorched by the summer's sun and pinched by the winter's cold, an instrument ordained to settle the wilderness."

From the depths of his indignation and hurt feelings Boone addressed a memorial to the Kentucky Legislature. In this he stated simply that until Indian troubles had ceased he had not attempted to settle down to farming, but had fought his country's fight; that then he had built his house and cleared his fields on land to which he supposed he had a perfect title. He ran over very briefly and modestly the sacrifices he had made in exploring, settling, and finally defending Kentucky. He complained of the injustice of acting under a complicated set of laws adopted long after his actual occupancy of the land. He asked for redress.

The plea remained unanswered. The men who were so unscrupulous as to "buy in" or locate the lands claimed by Boone were served by lawyers as sharp. They gained possession. Without doubt to-day their descendants talk proudly of their pioneer ancestors. Their names are on the records of the times. Suits of ejectment succeeded each other, one by one, until at the last Boone was left landless and almost penniless. Heartbroken, he packed his few belongings on his horses, and departed, abandoning his beloved Kentucky, vowing never again to dwell within her boundaries.

He headed for Point Pleasant, at the junction of the Great Kanawha and the Ohio rivers. Here, you will remember, was fought the great battle in the old days when the chief Cornstalk had led his men against the woodsmen under Lewis. Boone arrived here in 1788. For a time he kept a small store; and a little later we find him engaged in a great variety of occupations, guiding immigrants, surveying, supplying wild meat to the militia, and in just hunting. He was often far afield. Sometimes he even ventured north of the Ohio, where he had many narrow escapes from capture or death. The crack of his famous rifle was still dreaded by his old enemies. We hear of him at many widely separated places: visiting kinsfolk at the old Pennsylvania home, whither he and his wife and a son travelled on horseback; back at Maysville to settle some business; on the Monongahela River selling horses; at various points delivering ammunition and supplies to the militia in the field against the tormenting Indians. After Wayne's final crushing victory against the latter Boone for several seasons did almost nothing but hunt and trap. He gained particular renown for his success at beaver trapping. The game he killed he shared freely with the constantly increasing numbers of neighbours; the peltries he shipped to market.

For some years the valley of the Kanawha made him a good home. He was there greatly respected, which was balm to his bruised feelings. By popular petition he was appointed lieutenant-colonel of Kanawha County, and in many other ways the people accorded him marked distinction. Travellers journeyed long distances to see this man, distinguished throughout the western world, but nevertheless made homeless by his own state. One of these travellers has left an impression:

"His large head, full chest, square shoulders, and stout form are still impressed upon my mind. He was (I think) above five feet ten inches in height, and his weight say 175. He was solid in mind as well as in body, never frivolous, thoughtless, or agitated; but was always quiet, meditative, and impressive, unpretentious, kind and friendly in his manner. He came very much up to the idea we have of the old Grecian philosophers—particularly Diogenes."

Says another writer:

"I have often seen him get up early in the morning, walk hastily out, and look anxiously to the woods and snuff the autumnal winds with the highest rapture: and then return to the house and cast a quick and attentive look at the rifle, which was always suspended to a joist by a couple of buck horns or little forks. The hunting dog understanding the intentions of his master would wag his tail, and by every blandishment in his power express his readiness to accompany him to the woods."

However, in time the settlers began to be too numerous. The game was driven back. But especially the new type displeased Boone's placid and benevolent nature; the intense, nervous energy, the greed of some of them, the stinginess of others disturbed his hospitable soul.

One day two or three hunters came by Boone's cabin, and were, as a matter of course, made welcome. They stayed with him some time, hunting with him daytimes and sitting with him around the blazing fire in the evenings. They related to him adventures in far-off lands beyond the Mississippi; lands where the game roamed in vast herds, as in the Kentucky of yore; lands which the white man had seldom trod, and which the red man claimed by the strength of his good right arm; another Kentucky, unspoiled by the greeds of civilization. The old man's youth revived within him; his imagination was rekindled. At the age of sixty-five he resolved once more to set forth into the wilderness.

CHAPTER XXII

THE occasion of the setting forth from the Kanawha of Boone, his wife, and younger children must have warmed the old pioneer's heart. From far and near came the backwoodsmen and their families, by horseback, in canoe, on foot, until at Point Pleasant was an immense gathering to bid him farewell. It must have been a very touching occasion; for, as one writer expresses it, they "bade him farewell as solemnly affectionate as though he were departing for another world."

They set off in boats with all their household goods and as many of their domestic cattle as they could find room for. The journey was made by the waterways of the Ohio and Mississippi rivers, and was a leisurely affair. At all the little towns and stations they stopped to see friends or receive the heartfelt homage of the people, for Boone now found that, however officialdom might hurt him, the people loved and respected him. It was like a triumphal progress. After the settlements had been left behind nothing noteworthy happened, until at length the little flotilla landed on the Missouri banks of the Father of Waters.

All this part of the West was at that time under Spanish rule. Boone found the news of his coming had preceded him, and that even in advance of his arrival the Spanish governor had granted him a thousand acres of fine bottom-land on the Femme Osage Creek, adjoining land belonging to his son. Greatly soothed by this appreciation Boone here, with his own hands, built him a log cabin, and for the fourth time settled down as a pioneer.

The country was much to his liking. The inhabitants were scattered; game was abundant; the soil was rich; there were almost no taxes; and the only semblance of government was that vested in a single official called the *syndic,* who was a sort of combined judge, jury, military commander, and sheriff. To the west stretched the vast unknown plains full of Indians, wild animals, and wilder adventure. Boone resumed his old life with zest.

In this new country, too, the stability and solid worth of his character made themselves felt. By 1800 we see him appointed *syndic* for the whole district, truly a signal honour in a country ruled by the Spanish. So well did he perform all the duties of this composite office that when, by the Louisiana purchase, the United States took over the country, the French governor—you remember, possibly, that the country passed briefly from Spain through French hands—testified to President Jefferson's commissioner that, "Mr. Boone, a respectable old man, is just and impartial.

He has already, since I appointed him, offered his resignation owing to his infirmities, but believing I know his probity, I have induced him to remain, in view of my confidence in him, for the public good."

Boone knew nothing whatever about law, and his experience in Kentucky had not endeared it to him. In his court he had scant patience with technicalities and forms. But his sense of fairness and justice was keen, and his decisions, says Thwaites, "based solely on common-sense in the rough, were respected as if coming from the supreme bench." The same writer says: "His methods were as primitive and arbitrary as those of an oriental pasha; his penalties frequently consisted of lashes on the bare back 'well laid on'; he would observe no rules of evidence, saying he wished only to know the truth; and sometimes both parties to a suit were compelled to divide the costs and begone. During his four years of office he passed on the disputes of his neighbours with such absolute fairness as to win popular approbation." Another of the duties of his office, which the old man greatly relished, was showing immigrants to desirable tracts of land. No one could have been better fitted for that. His hunting expeditions taught him the country; his keen practised eye was always on the alert for fertile soil and favourable location. In addition, his contemporaries all say, the duty possessed in Boone's eyes a quality of hospitality that vastly appealed to him. He was showing his guests around. The universal testimony from those who have left personal testimony is that at this task Boone was

at his best, displaying a charming simple dignity that
quieted the roughest men and captured the affections of all
with whom he came in contact.

In the interims between official duties he was as active as
ever in the field, despite his advancing years. His eyesight
was failing somewhat, so that he complains that the old un-
erring marksmanship was no longer quite at his command.
Nevertheless, he could still outshoot most of his neighbours,
and his skill as a trapper of fur was unexcelled. Chiefly
he sought beaver skins, which he could then sell in St. Louis
for nine dollars each. He has himself said that, with the
exception of his first years in the new Kentucky, this was the
happiest period of his life.

Many travellers made it a point to visit the famous Scout
and a number have left their impressions of him. Even
after the age of seventy he was evidently a vigorous man.
Audubon the naturalist says: "The stature and general appearance of this wanderer of the western parts approached
the gigantic. His chest was broad and prominent, his muscular powers displayed themselves in every limb; his countenance gave indication of his great courage, enterprise, and
persistence; and when he spoke the very motion of his lips
brought the impression that whatever he uttered could not
be otherwise than strictly true." Even at this period, when
Boone was lamenting the waning of his marksmanship,
Audubon testifies: "We had returned from a shooting excursion, in the course of which his extraordinary skill in
the management of the rifle had been fully displayed."

But this ideal existence was not long to continue. In 1804 the United States took over by purchase the whole of this country. Naturally Boone's authority as a Spanish magistrate ended with that fact. This was not serious, but what followed was. The grants of land made to Boone by the Spanish governor were shortly found to be faulty. The old man should have journeyed to New Orleans in person to fulfil certain red-tape obligations. The journey required would have been a thousand miles by waterway between banks swarming with Indians; and a return by land—the current was too fast for a return by water—through the same foes. The local Spanish governor assured Boone that he, as *syndic,* need not fulfil this law; and the old man, believing his informant, never made the journey. We are informed that the land commissioners, "while highly respecting him, were regretfully obliged" to deprive him of his land. Again Boone found himself made landless by his own country. On the advice of friends he sent in memorials to both the Kentucky Legislature and Congress, but only six years later did Congress at length take action to confirm his Spanish grant.

In the meantime, the old Scout, unembittered by the essential injustice of this calamity, took up with renewed vigour the life of a fur trapper. He made long trips into the wilderness, into hostile country, almost alone. They would have been extraordinary trips for any man, but when we consider Boone's advanced age, we cannot but wonder. At the age of eighty, for example, we hear of him in the

Yellowstone! Sometimes one of his sons accompanied him, but most often his only companion was an old Indian.

In those days the fur trade was a very paying business. Indeed, it was about at this period that the great companies were solidifying their immense influence, and such fortunes as that of John Jacob Astor were made. Trappers were either "company men," or "free trappers." The former were paid regular salaries and of course turned over to their employers all their skins; the latter were supplied with traps and ammunition and turned loose to wander at their own wills, it being understood that they sell their catch to the company that had supplied them, at a price agreed upon beforehand. The outfit consisted generally of two or three horses, one for riding and the others for packing the simple camp outfits and the furs. It was of course very desirable to find, if possible, regions unvisited by either white man or Indian; and in consequence long and solitary journeys were the rule.

Your trapper was in those days a highly considered individual. He led a bold, free life, and his adventures struck hard at the imagination. He thought rather well of himself and of his calling; and he dressed the part. His buckskin clothes, fragrant with smoke tan, were fringed and embroidered heavily with porcupine quills stained in bright colours. His moccasins especially were often real works of art. Customarily, he wore a flexible felt hat, as successor to the old coon-skin cap usual in the more wooded countries.

Early in the spring, just as soon as the ice had melted in the mountain streams, he arrived at his trapping grounds. Carefully he followed up the beds of the watercourses, watching on either bank for signs of any of the valuable fur-bearing animals. Every down tree he examined to see if by chance a beaver might have cut it down; and if such proved to be the case, whether the animal had felled it for food or as material for a dam. Every beaver track he followed to determine whether it might not lead to a runway where he could set his trap. When he came to a beaver house, he set his trap at the edge of the dam just where the beaver, coming out from deep water, first set his foot into shoal. Once the traps were all set the busy routine life began. The "circle" of traps often involved a journey of many miles. On his return from the circle, our trapper had next to skin his catch, stretch the skins over hoops of willow, and then painstakingly to scrape and pare them free from flesh and fat. His food during the trapping season was "jerked" meat and what provisions he had brought with him. All the meat for his use he had killed and dried before coming on the trapping grounds; for, if he could avoid it, the sound of a rifle must not be heard in the fur country. Beaver tails, however, which were considered a great dainty, gave him the variety of fresh meat.

A book called "Buxton's Travels" gives an interesting picture of this life:

"During the hunt, regardless of Indian vicinity, the fearless trapper wanders far and near in search of 'sign.' His nerves must ever be in a state of tension and his mind ever present at his call.   His eagle eye sweeps around the country, and in an instant detects any foreign appearance.   A turned leaf, a blade of grass pressed down, the uneasiness of wild animals, the flight of birds, are all paragraphs to him written in Nature's legible hand and plainest language. All the wits of the subtle savage are called into play to gain an advantage over the wily woodsman; but with the instinct of the primitive man, the white hunter has the advantage of a civilized mind, and thus provided seldom fails to outwit, under equal advantages, the cunning savage.

"Sometimes the Indian following on his trail watches him set his traps on a shrub-belted stream, and passing up the bed, like Bruce of old, so that he may leave no track, he lies in wait in the bushes until the hunter comes to examine. Then waiting until he approaches his ambush within a few feet, whiz flies the home-drawn arrow, never failing at such close quarters to bring the victim to the ground.   For one white scalp, however, that dangles in the smoke of an Indian lodge a dozen black ones at the end of the hunt ornament the campfire of the rendezvous.

"At a certain time when the hunt is over, or they have loaded their pack animals, the trappers proceed to their rendezvous, the locality of which has been previously agreed upon; and here the traders and agents of the fur companies await them, with such assortments of goods as their hardy customers may require, including generally a fair supply of alcohol.   The trappers drop in singly and in small bands, bringing their packs of beaver to this mountain market, not unfrequently to the value of a thousand dollars each, the produce of one hunt. The dissipation of the rendezvous, however, soon turns the trapper's pocket inside out. The goods brought by the traders, although of the most inferior quality, are sold at enormous prices. Coffee twenty and thirty shillings a pint cup, which is the usual measure; tobacco fetches ten and fifteen shillings a plug; alcohol from twenty to fifty shillings a pint; gunpowder sixteen shillings a pint cup, and all other articles at proportionately exorbitant prices.

"The rendezvous is one continued scene of drunkenness, gambling, brawling and fighting, so long as the money and credit of the trappers last. Seated Indian fashion around the fires, with a blanket spread before them, groups are seen with their 'decks' of cards playing at 'euchre,' 'poker,' and 'seven-up,' the regular mountain games. The stakes are beaver, which is here current coin; and when the fur is gone, their horses, mules, rifles and shirts, hunting packs and breeches are staked. Daring gamblers make the rounds of the camp, challenging each other to play for the highest stake—his horse, his squaw if he have one, and as once happened his scalp. A trapper often squanders the produce of his hunt, amounting to hundreds of dollars, in a couple of hours, and, supplied on credit with another equipment, leaves the rendezvous for another expedition which has the same result, time after time, although one tolerably successful hunt would enable him to return to the settlements and civilized life with an ample sum to purchase and stock a farm, and enjoy himself in ease and comfort for the remainder of his days.

"These annual gatherings are often the scene of bloody duels, for over their cups and cards no men are more quarrelsome than your mountaineers. Rifles at twenty paces settle all differences, and as may be imagined, the fall of one or the other of the combatants is certain, or, as sometimes happens, both fall at the same fire."

This life Daniel Boone lived, all but the carousals and squanderings at the rendezvous. He saved his makings and brought them home. He was now getting to be an old man; in spite of the robustness of his constitution these long and perilous journeys were beginning to tell on him. On one occasion he was taken so dangerously sick that it seemed to him he must certainly die. For a long time he lay in camp unable to move, while a storm raged. Finally a pleasant day came when he felt able to walk. Leaning heavily on a stick he struggled to the top of a small hill and there, with the point of his staff, he marked out his grave. Then he proceeded to give his companion, who this time happened to be merely a negro boy of twelve years, the most careful instructions. He told him, in case the illness proved fatal, to "wash and lay his body straight, wrapped up in one of the cleanest blankets. He was then to construct a kind of shovel, and with that instrument and the hatchet to dig a grave exactly as he had marked it out. He was then to drag the body to the place and put it in the grave, which he was directed to cover up, putting posts at head and foot. Poles were to be placed around and above the surface, the trees to be marked so the place could be easily found by his friends; the horses were to be caught, the blankets and skins gathered up, with especial instructions about the old rifle, and various messages to his family. All these directions were given, as the boy afterwards declared, with entire calmness, and as if he were giving instructions about ordinary business." Fortunately he recovered: but he broke camp and returned home without attempting to continue the hunting.

Another incident Abbott quotes from some unnamed writer as follows:

"One writer says Colonel Boone went on a trapping excursion up the Grand River. This stream rises in the southern part of Iowa, and flows in a southerly course into the Missouri. He was entirely alone. Paddling his canoe up the lonely banks of the Missouri, he entered the Grand River, and established his camp in a silent sheltered cove, where an experienced hunter would with difficulty find it.

"Here he first laid in his supply of venison, turkeys, and bear's meat, and then commenced his trapping operation, where no sound of his rifle would disturb the beavers and no smell of gunpowder would excite their alarm. Every morning he took the circuit of his traps, visiting them all in turn. Much to his alarm, he one morning encountered a large encampment of Indians in his vicinity engaged in hunting. He immediately retreated to his camp and secreted himself. Fortunately for him, quite a deep snow fell that night, which covered his traps. But this same snow prevented him from leaving his camp, lest his footprints should be discovered. For twenty days he continued thus secreted, occasionally, at midnight, venturing to cook a little food, when there was no danger that the smoke of his fire would reveal his retreat. At length the enemy departed, and he was released from his long imprisonment. He subsequently stated that never in his life had he felt so much anxiety for so long a period lest the Indians should discover his traps and search out his camp."

In vain his family tried to keep him at least somewhere near home. Their appeals made no impression on the old man. At length they did manage to persuade him never to go anywhere without the Indian before mentioned. The latter was solemnly instructed to bring the Colonel back "dead or alive."

It was only in 1810 that the reason for the old gentleman's persistence became clear. Again he set forth on a long and perilous journey, but this time with his face to the east. Once more he stood within the borders of Kentucky.

It seems that the lang-grabbing sharks and pettifogging lawyers had not only cleaned him out of land but the defense of the lawsuits had left him in debt. Those who stood his creditors had never by word or deed reminded him of that fact, nor was it known except to them and to Boone. Such was the esteem in which he was held that no one, as far as could be learned, had the slightest notion of ever pressing the matter. But that did not help Boone's standing with himself. By the most incredible exertions, in his old age, he had managed to get the money; and now he journeyed from place to place, saw every creditor, and paid in full. Then he travelled back to his family, satisfied. This excursion left him of all his wealth just one fifty-cent piece! But Boone was exultant.

"Now," he cried, "I am ready and willing to die! I am relieved from a burden which has long oppressed me. I have paid all my debts, and no one can say when I am gone, 'Boone was a dishonest man.' I am perfectly content now to die."

THE NEW FRONTIER

CHAPTER XXIII

THE War ot 1812 was fought. Boone chafed like a young man over the refusal of the authorities to permit him to enlist! He was then seventy-eight years old. His impatience rose to a very high pitch when the uneasiness of the war farther east brought on Indian troubles nearer at home. Some of the farm property of the younger members of the Boone family was destroyed in one of these raids, and Boone's sons, Daniel Morgan and Nathan, were leaders of the troops sent out in reprisal. A year later Boone's wife died, a great grief, as she had been since early youth his heroic companion.

Mrs. Boone's death, combined with his penniless condition, induced the old Scout to abandon his separate establishment and to join the household of his son, Nathan. The latter seems to have been a worthy descendant of the old stock.   He was first a hunter and explorer, then a very successful farmer on what was then a large scale.   In the British War of 1812 he served with great distinction.   The military life seems to have suited him well, for at the close of the war he remained in the regular army where he soon gained the rank of lieutenant-colonel.   Most of his campaigning was among the Indians comparatively near home, and in this fighting he had many thrilling adventures.   The farmhouse he built was of stone, two storied, on substantial Colonial lines, and of truly mansion size and architecture.   Here the old Scout took up his quarters, still chafing at the thought that he had no part in the war.

Immediately at its cessation, however, he started off on a hunting trip, "just to show them."   He was heard of at Fort Osage on his way to the Platte "in the dress of the roughest, poorest hunter."   When winter shut down he reluctantly returned.   There were too many immigrants coming in to suit Boone's taste: they were slowly filling up the land and driving the game back.   Also there was too much law court, politics, land grabs, and speculation.   In spite of his now great age Boone seriously talked of moving again still farther west to make a fresh start!   He was talked out of this by his sons and neighbours; but he insisted on fixing up part of an old log blockhouse as quarters to which he could at least temporarily escape.   His life was still active.   In the summer he kept busy working on the farms of his children or chopping down trees for the winter's firewood.   In the evenings nothing delighted him more than to gather at his fireside a group of men who could tell him of things "hid beyond the ranges." He was intensely interested in the Rocky Mountains, then on the edge of exploration, and eagerly questioned everybody who could give him the least knowledge of California. Indeed it is said that his fresh enthusiasm was the cause of several young men's migrating to the Pacific Coast. "A tale of new lands ever found in him a delighted listener."

But more often those who sat around the fire themselves played the part of listeners while the old Scout sought in his recollections for amusing or thrilling tales. The Boone farm was visited by many people who came for the sole purpose of seeing the celebrated frontiersman. Among them were many men of distinction. Boone received them all with his fine simplicity, but it is pleasant to think that this attention from men, themselves of celebrity, must have pleased him. One of these visitors leaves this impression of him, by which it can be seen that age was still sitting lightly on his head.

"He was of a very erect, clean-limbed, and athletic form —admirably fitted in structure, muscle, temperament, and habit for the labours, changes, and sufferings he underwent. He had what phrenologists would have considered a model head—with a forehead peculiarly high, noble, and bold—thin and compressed lips—a mild, clear blue eye—a large and prominent chin, and a general expression of countenance in which fearlessness and courage sat enthroned."

Another says:

"He was of very mild countenance, fair complexion, soft and quiet in his manner, but little to say unless spoken to, amiable and kind in his feelings, very fond of quiet retirement, of cool self-possession, and indomitable perseverance."

Mind you this last was written of him when he was eighty-four years old. The following year, when he was eighty-five, Chester Harding writes that he found him "living alone in a cabin, a part of an old blockhouse," roasting a venison steak on the end of his ramrod. Harding speaks with great admiration of the accuracy of his memory and the vividness yet modesty of his narratives.

"I asked him," writes Harding, "if he never got lost in his long wanderings after game. He said, 'No, I was never lost, *but I was bewildered once for three days.*'"

But when the haze of autumn spread over the land and the smell of wood smoke filled the air, Boone always got restless. With his Indian companion he would disappear for weeks at a time. At the age of eighty-four he wrote one of his sons: "I intend by next summer to take two or three whites and a party of Osage Indians to visit the salt mountains, lakes, and ponds and see these natural curiosities. They are about five or six hundred miles west of here."

But it is very doubtful if this expedition ever came off. Boone's eyesight was now so bad that he had to attach pieces of white paper to his rifle sights; but his nerves were unpalsied, and what he could see he could still hit. Doubtless the venison Harding found him roasting on the end of the ramrod was of his own killing. He was content. A contemporary says that "at this period of his life an irritable expression never escaped his lips."

Says another:

"His personal appearance was venerable and attractive, very neatly clad in garments spun, woven, and made in the cabins. His countenance was pleasant, calm, and fair, his forehead high and bold, and the soft silver of his hair in unison with his length of days. He spoke, feelingly and with solemnity, of being a creature of Providence, ordained by Heaven as a pioneer in the wilderness to advance the civilization and the extension of his country. He professed the belief that the Almighty had assigned to him a work to perform, and that he had only followed the pathway of duty in the work he had pursued; that he had discharged his duty to God and his country by following the direction of Providence."

His children and grandchildren adored him, and surrounded him with affectionate attentions. Then, too, he was much cheered by the fact that at last Congress, after years of delay, had voted to confirm his Spanish grant of land. It was now too late to do the old man any good; but it comforted him greatly to feel that he had something substantial to leave his children. Not that they needed it: but it was a matter that touched the old gentleman's pride.

No longer was he able to do the heavy work of the farm, nor go far afield in his hunting expeditions; but still his active nature was as busy as ever, though in a different way. He was an expert at repairing rifles, for instance, and could make and carve the most beautiful powder horns; or could manufacture moccasins, hunting shirts, or snowshoes. These things he did for his neighbours out of the generosity of his heart. Except for the partial dimming of his eyesight, his health and vigour remained good to the last. He died at his son Nathan's house when eighty-six years of age after only three days of illness.

Drawing a moral is a priggish thing to do. Such a life speaks for itself. Yet one cannot help asking oneself why Boone's fame stands out so predominantly above the other forest men of his time. George Rogers Clark, for example, with his bold, picturesque, and successful campaigns would seem to have performed greater military service to the struggling settlements; Simon Kenton had as thrilling adventures. The answer is, in character. The picture that persists at the last is not the smoke and dust of battle and combat, but the figure of a serene, unworldly, kindly soul, fronting what fate brought him, whether of peace or of turmoil, with spirit unruffled and unafraid.

THE END

9 780766 170353